CALA TRAVEL GUIDE

2024 Edition

Calabria Escapades: A Journey Through Time, Nature, and Flavor in the Enchanting Land of Calabria

By

Williams Carter

TABLE OF CONTENT

CHAPTER THREE

CHAPTER FOUR

CHAPTER FIVE

CALABRIA'S RICH CULTURAL HERITAGE
5.1 FOLK MUSIC AND DANCE: A CELEBRATION OF LIFE
5.2 THE ART OF HANDICRAFTS: LOCAL ARTISANS AT WORK
5.3 RELIGIOUS FESTIVALS: EMBRACING TRADITION AND FAITH

CHAPTER SIX

INDULGING IN CALABRIAN CUISINE
6.1 A GASTRONOMIC JOURNEY: TASTING CALABRIA'S FLAVORS
6.2 MUST-TRY DISHES: FROM 'NDUJA TO CUZZUPA
6.3 LOCAL WINE AND LIQUORS: TOASTING TO THE GOOD LIFE

CHAPTER SEVEN

OUTDOOR ACTIVITIES AND ADVENTURE
7.1 HIKING AND TREKKING: TRAILS OF BEAUTY AND CHALLENGE
7.1.1 Coastal Walks: Exploring the Tyrrhenian and Ionian Shores
7.1.2 Mountain Treks: Scaling the Peaks of Sila and Aspromonte
7.1.3 Pilgrim Routes: Spiritual Hiking Trails
7.2 WATER SPORTS: DIVING, SAILING, AND BEYOND
7.2.1 Diving Adventures: Beneath the Azure Surface
7.2.2 Sailing and Yachting: Navigating the Calabrian Coast
7.2.3 Windsurfing and Kitesurfing: Harnessing the Wind's Energy
7.3 RURAL ESCAPES: FARM STAYS AND AGRITOURISM
7.3.1 Farm Stays: Authentic Rural Living
7.3.2 Culinary Tours: Tasting the Bounty of the Land
7.3.3 Cultural Immersion: Embracing Local Traditions

CHAPTER EIGHT

IMPORTANT NOTE BEFORE READING

You might find a special trip experience in these pages.

The purpose of this Calabria travel guide is to inspire your creativity, imagination, and sense of adventure. Since we think that the beauty of every discovery should be experienced firsthand, free from visual filter and prejudices, you won't find any pictures here. Every monument, every location, and every secret nook are waiting for you when you get there, eager to surprise and amaze you. Why should we ruin the wonder and excitement of the initial impression? Prepare to set off on a voyage where your imagination will serve as both your single mode of transportation and your personal tour guide. Keep in mind that your own creations are the most attractive.

This book lacks a map and photographs, in contrast to many other manuals. Why? Because in our opinion the best discoveries are made when a person gets lost, lets themselves go with the flow of the environment, and embraces the ambiguity of the road.

Be cautious, trust your gut, and expect the unexpected. In a world without maps, where roads are made with each step you take, the magic of the voyage starts now.

INTRODUCTION

Unraveling the Enigma of Calabria:

Calabria, situated in the southernmost region of Italy, has long remained an enigmatic and captivating destination, beckoning travelers and historians alike with its alluring mystique. As the toe of Italy's boot, this beguiling region stands at the crossroads of ancient civilizations, each leaving their indelible mark on its storied landscape. From the moment one sets foot on its shores, Calabria weaves a spell that transcends time, inviting visitors to immerse themselves in its rich tapestry of history, culture, and natural beauty.

At the heart of Calabria's allure are its breathtaking landscapes that range from the majestic peaks of the Sila Mountains to the sun-kissed shores of the Tyrrhenian and Ionian Seas. Verdant valleys, dotted with quaint villages and olive groves, complement the azure coastline, creating a visual symphony that captivates the soul. Nestled amid these diverse landscapes are the echoes of ancient civilizations that have called Calabria home, each layer contributing to the region's cultural mosaic.

As we embark on our journey through Calabria, we step into a world where time seems to slow down, allowing us to savor every moment and uncover the hidden gems that lay scattered throughout. From historic towns adorned with architectural marvels to time-worn castles that guard the secrets of the past, the essence of Calabria is a story waiting to be told.

As travelers traverse the sunlit countryside and explore the narrow cobblestone streets, they encounter a warm and vibrant culture, imbibed with traditions passed down through generations. The proud people of Calabria, known for their hospitality and sense of community, are eager to share their heritage, traditions, and delectable cuisine with open hearts and welcoming smiles.

The region's past is an intricate patchwork of influences, bearing the footprints of the Greeks, Romans, Byzantines, and Normans, among others. With every archaeological site and historical monument, Calabria reveals fragments of its past, offering a glimpse into the lives of those who once thrived in these ancient lands.

Beyond the historical grandeur, Calabria's cultural legacy is alive in its vibrant festivals, where age-old customs blend seamlessly with modern celebrations. From the boisterous Carnivals that fill the streets with color and music to the solemn processions honoring patron saints, these events reveal the profound connection between the past and the present.

As we peel back the layers of mystery that shroud this unique region, we embark on a journey of discovery, guided by the whispers of history and the embrace of its people. Calabria's allure lies not only in its breathtaking landscapes and Mediterranean charm but also in the tapestry of culture and heritage that weaves an enchanting tale. With each step, we uncover a treasure trove of hidden wonders, each inviting us to partake in the enduring enchantment that is Calabria.

A Brief History of Calabria's Cultural Legacy:

The history of Calabria unfolds like a captivating tapestry, intricately woven by the threads of numerous ancient civilizations that have left their indelible marks on this diverse and enchanting region. Among the earliest to grace its shores were the ancient Greeks, who settled in Magna Graecia, establishing flourishing colonies that thrived amidst the bountiful natural beauty of the land. Their legacy can still be witnessed in the remnants of ancient temples, amphitheaters, and majestic ruins scattered across the landscape.

The Romans, renowned for their engineering prowess and administrative acumen, followed in the footsteps of the Greeks, leaving behind an impressive array of grand structures that stand as enduring testaments to their once-mighty empire. Magnificent aqueducts, bridges, and amphitheaters bear witness to the golden era of Roman rule in Calabria, showcasing their remarkable contributions to the region's architecture and infrastructure.

The Byzantine Empire, with its rich cultural heritage and influence, also made its mark on Calabria during the Middle Ages. The presence of Byzantine settlers shaped the region's artistic, religious, and societal aspects. Splendid monasteries, adorned with intricate mosaics and frescoes, emerged as centers of spiritual and cultural life, their presence adding to the region's profound artistic heritage.

As we traverse through time in Calabria's historical narrative, we bear witness to the intermingling of cultures that have contributed to the development of the region's unique identity. The mosaic of influences is reflected not only in its architectural wonders but also in the local language, traditions, and customs that have been passed down through generations.

Calabria's distinct dialect, infused with ancient Greek and Latin elements, stands as a testament to the region's rich linguistic heritage, serving as a linguistic bridge to its ancient past. The warmth and hospitality of its inhabitants are also a reflection of the diverse cultures that have called this land home, making every visitor feel welcomed and embraced.

Journeying through Calabria, one encounters medieval castles perched atop hilltops, stoically guarding the secrets of centuries past. These fortresses are silent witnesses to the region's tumultuous history, bearing the scars of conquests, battles, and moments of triumph.

Moreover, the land itself is adorned with archaeological sites that seem to transport travelers back in time. Ancient cities and ruins offer glimpses into the lives of past civilizations, and the whispers of the past resonate through the ages, inviting us to connect with the experiences and aspirations of those who walked these lands long before us.

The history of Calabria is an evolving narrative that continues to inspire awe and wonder. It is a story of resilience, creativity, and the harmonious fusion of diverse cultures. As we delve deeper into its historical legacy, we are rewarded with an enriched understanding of Calabria's vibrant past, a past that breathes life into the present and shapes the future of this captivating and ever-evolving region.

Why Calabria is Italy's Best-Kept Secret:

Despite its undeniable allure and rich cultural heritage, Calabria has often remained overlooked by mass tourism, earning its reputation as Italy's best-kept secret. While other regions of Italy might bask in the limelight, Calabria quietly captivates those intrepid travelers who venture off the beaten path seeking an authentic and unspoiled experience.

The secret to Calabria's allure lies in its untouched beauty and the genuine warmth of its people. The region's natural wonders, from the rugged Sila National Park to the pristine beaches along the Ionian and Tyrrhenian coasts, offer an escape into untouched landscapes. Its traditional festivals, celebrated with infectious joy and devotion, showcase a side of Italian culture that transcends the stereotypical portrayals.

As we journey deeper into the heart of Calabria, we'll uncover the essence of its best-kept secret: its ability to charm and captivate, leaving an indelible mark on the souls of those fortunate enough to discover its hidden treasures. With each turn, we'll come to understand why Calabria remains an alluring enigma and a place of enchantment, destined to capture the hearts of travelers seeking genuine experiences in the heart of Southern Italy.

CHAPTER ONE

Getting to Know Calabria

1.1 Geography and Climate: From Mountains to Sea

Calabria's diverse and captivating landscape is one of its most defining features. Nestled in the southernmost part of Italy, this picturesque region stretches from the rugged mountains of the Apennines to the sparkling waters of the Tyrrhenian and Ionian Seas. As you traverse the area, you'll be enchanted by the ever-changing scenery, each corner offering a unique blend of natural beauty.

1.1.1 The Majestic Apennines: Calabria's Mountainous Heart

Venture inland, and you'll find yourself on an awe-inspiring journey into the heart of Calabria's majestic Apennine Mountains. This central landscape of rugged peaks and verdant valleys offers a captivating escape for nature lovers and adventure seekers alike. Among these magnificent mountains, the Sila mountain range, affectionately known as "La Sila," stands out as a true gem, offering an unparalleled experience in the embrace of unspoiled beauty.

The Enchanting Beauty of La Sila

Nestled within the Calabrian Apennines, the Sila mountain range is a natural wonder that beckons travelers to immerse themselves in its tranquil ambiance. As you ascend into La Sila's realm, a world of enchantment unfolds before your eyes, where time seems to slow down, and the modern world's hustle and bustle fades away.

Serene Lakes and Alpine Charms

La Sila boasts a series of picturesque lakes that mirror the sky's hues and create a sense of serenity that transcends the ordinary. Lake Ampollino, Lake Arvo, and Lake Cecita are among the most captivating, reflecting the surrounding mountains and lush forests like sparkling gems in a verdant crown. The alpine villages scattered throughout the region add to the charm, with their quaint architecture and warm hospitality welcoming visitors with open arms.

Embrace Nature's Sanctuary: Dense Forests and Wildlife

Within the embrace of La Sila, dense forests thrive, blanketing the mountains in a lush carpet of green. This natural sanctuary is home to a diverse array of wildlife, including foxes, deer, and rare bird species, creating an ecosystem that enthralls nature enthusiasts and photographers alike. Birdwatching becomes a delightful pursuit as you listen to the melodic songs of various avian residents that call La Sila their home.

The Call of Adventure: Hiking and Scenic Trails

For those with an adventurous spirit, La Sila presents an inviting network of hiking trails that meander through its mesmerizing landscapes. Traverse these paths, and you'll find yourself amidst breathtaking panoramas, where snow-capped peaks and azure skies form an enchanting tapestry. Whether you're an experienced hiker seeking a challenging ascent or a leisurely stroller in search of tranquility, La Sila's trails cater to all levels of exploration.

Winter Wonderland: Snow-capped Beauty

During the winter months, La Sila transforms into a snow-kissed wonderland, offering a haven for snow sports enthusiasts. Skiing, snowboarding, and sledding become favorite pastimes as the mountains don their winter mantle. Winter festivals and charming Christmas markets add to the region's allure, inviting you to partake in the joyful celebrations of the season.

Unveiling Historical Treasures

Beyond its natural splendor, La Sila also holds traces of its historical heritage. As you wander through the region, you may stumble upon ancient monasteries and churches, bearing witness to centuries of spiritual significance and cultural richness.

Embrace the thrill of exploration in the majestic Apennines of Calabria's La Sila, where each step draws you deeper into a world of wonder and discovery. Whether you seek adventure, serenity, or an intimate connection with nature, this cherished mountain range will leave an indelible mark on your heart, inviting you to return time and time again to experience its boundless magic.

1.1.2 The Enchanting Coastlines: Sun-Kissed Beaches and Charming Coves

Descend towards the coast, and you'll be greeted by a breathtaking sight that will captivate your senses – the alluring coastline of Calabria that stretches for miles along both the Tyrrhenian and Ionian Seas. With its pristine beaches, hidden coves, and crystal-clear waters, Calabria's coastal beauty is a treasure trove waiting to be explored, offering a diverse range of experiences for every traveler's delight.

Vibrant Beaches: Tropea and Capo Vaticano

As you reach the Tyrrhenian coast, prepare to be dazzled by the vibrant beaches that have made Calabria a sought-after destination. Tropea, with its postcard-perfect setting atop a cliff, invites you to relax on its sandy shores while gazing at the turquoise waters below. Wander through the charming streets of this coastal gem, savoring the delectable seafood dishes and gelato that are synonymous with Italian coastal living. Nearby, the promontory of Capo Vaticano unveils secluded bays and sweeping vistas, offering a paradise for nature lovers and those seeking tranquility.

The Enchanting Charms of Scilla

Venturing further south, you'll encounter the coastal town of Scilla, nestled along the Tyrrhenian Sea. Its enchanting beaches and the imposing Ruffo Castle overlooking the sea create an ethereal atmosphere that has inspired legends and myths throughout the ages. Stroll through the colorful fishing village, where the aroma of fresh seafood fills the air, and visit the Chianalea district, known for its picturesque houses built directly on the water's edge. Scilla's spellbinding beauty leaves an indelible impression on every visitor.

Diamante: A Hidden Gem

On the Tyrrhenian coast, the charming town of Diamante awaits discovery. Known as the "City of Murals," Diamante's streets and alleys are adorned with vibrant and artistic frescoes that showcase the town's cultural vibrancy. Beyond its artistic allure, Diamante boasts delightful beaches and scenic spots where you can savor the stunning views and soak in the Mediterranean sunshine.

A Haven for Water Sports Enthusiasts

For those seeking an adrenaline rush, Calabria's coastline offers an array of thrilling water sports. Windsurfing, kiteboarding, and sailing enthusiasts will find the conditions perfect for indulging in their favorite activities. The Ionian coast, in particular, is renowned for its steady winds, attracting windsurfers from around the world to ride its waves. Dive into the azure waters, and you'll discover an underwater wonderland teeming with marine life, making snorkeling and scuba diving memorable experiences.

Sunset Magic and Evening Strolls

As the day draws to a close, prepare for one of Calabria's most magical moments – the sunset over the sea. Find a vantage point along the coast, and watch as the sun dips below the horizon, painting the sky in a kaleidoscope of colors. These tranquil moments create an ambiance of serenity, making the perfect backdrop for a leisurely evening stroll along the shore.

In Calabria, the coastal charm is both invigorating and serene, beckoning travelers to embrace its beauty in their own way. Whether you're seeking relaxation on idyllic beaches, immersing yourself in local culture, or embarking on thrilling water adventures, Calabria's coastal allure promises an unforgettable experience that will stay with you long after you've bid farewell to its shores.

1.1.3 Climate and Seasons: Embracing Nature's Rhythms

The climate of Calabria is a beautiful symphony of diversity, mirroring the region's captivating landscape. From the sun-drenched coastlines to the refreshing mountain retreats, each area boasts its own distinct weather patterns, creating an enticing tapestry of climates that cater to a wide array of preferences and activities.

Mediterranean Magic: Coastal Climate

Along the glistening shores of the Tyrrhenian and Ionian Seas, Calabria basks in a classic Mediterranean climate that exudes warmth and vitality. During the long, sun-drenched summers, the coastal areas are blessed with abundant sunshine, infusing the region with energy and drawing visitors to its sandy beaches and inviting waters. The sun-kissed days create the perfect ambiance for seaside relaxation, water sports, and coastal adventures.

Hot Summers, Perfect for Fun in the Sun

In the coastal towns and cities, summer unfolds in a blaze of brilliance, with temperatures reaching their peak. Days are characterized by clear skies and temperatures that often climb into the high 80s to low 90s Fahrenheit (30-35 degrees Celsius). Tourists and locals alike flock to the beaches to soak up the Mediterranean sun, enjoy refreshing dips in the sea, and indulge in leisurely beachside activities.

Mild, Refreshing Winters

As the summer heat recedes, autumn transitions into a milder season that embraces the coastline with its gentle touch. Winter follows with its mild and rainy character, providing a refreshing respite from the summer warmth. The winter months experience average temperatures ranging from the mid-50s to low 60s Fahrenheit (12-16 degrees Celsius), offering a pleasant climate for exploring coastal towns, historic sites, and enjoying the region's renowned culinary delights.

Mountain Mystique: Cool Summer Escapes

Venturing inland towards the majestic Apennines, the climate takes on a different personality. The mountainous regions of Calabria experience cooler temperatures compared to the coastal areas, making them an inviting escape during the scorching summer months. The Sila mountain range, in particular, offers a cool refuge where visitors can relish temperatures that rarely rise above the mid-70s Fahrenheit (around 24 degrees Celsius) during the height of summer.

Winter Wonderland in the Mountains

When winter comes, the mountain peaks of Sila and other ranges in Calabria transform into a picturesque winter wonderland. Snow blankets the landscape, turning the region into a paradise for winter sports enthusiasts and those seeking a magical winter retreat. Ski resorts come alive, attracting snowboarders, skiers, and families eager to experience the thrill of winter sports amid stunning mountain panoramas.

Calabria's diverse climate is a blessing, as it allows visitors to curate their experiences based on personal preferences and interests. Whether you seek sun-soaked coastal adventures or a refreshing mountain getaway, Calabria's varied climate ensures that every season holds the promise of unforgettable moments and cherished memories in this idyllic corner of Southern Italy.

1.2 The Unique Character of Calabrian People

Calabria's people, known as Calabrians, are a warm, resilient, and deeply proud community. Rooted in a rich tapestry of history and cultural influences, their character is shaped by the region's past, present challenges, and unwavering spirit.

1.2.1 Resilience and Traditions: Navigating Life's Challenges

Calabrians have endured a remarkable journey through history, marked by trials and tribulations that have tested the resilience of their spirit. From ancient invasions to devastating natural disasters and economic struggles, the people of Calabria have faced adversity with an unwavering resolve and a strong sense of community that has fortified their identity and preserved their cherished traditions.

A Tapestry of Resilience: History's Trials

The annals of Calabria's history are woven with stories of perseverance and courage. Throughout the centuries, the region experienced waves of conquests and invasions by various civilizations, including the Greeks, Romans, Byzantines, Normans, and others. These tumultuous events shaped the cultural fabric of Calabria, leaving an indelible mark on its people. Despite facing foreign rule and the challenges of assimilation, Calabrians tenaciously held on to their distinct identity, languages, and customs.

Nature's Fury: Triumph over Natural Disasters

Calabria is no stranger to the wrath of nature. The region has witnessed earthquakes, volcanic eruptions, and devastating floods that have tested the resolve of its inhabitants. Yet, through each tragedy, Calabrians have displayed remarkable resilience, joining forces as a community to rebuild their homes and lives. Their ability to find strength in unity has been a key factor in overcoming the aftermath of natural calamities and paving the way for the region's recovery.

Enduring Economic Struggles: A Journey to Prosperity

Throughout its history, Calabria has faced economic challenges, with periods of poverty and hardship affecting the livelihoods of its people. However, the determination and ingenuity of Calabrians have led to the development of sustainable solutions and innovative industries. Agriculture, artisanal crafts, and tourism have emerged as pillars of the local economy, allowing the region to harness its cultural heritage and natural beauty as valuable assets for economic growth.

Embracing Heritage: A Symphony of Tradition

Amidst the challenges, the spirit of Calabria finds expression in its rich tapestry of traditions and cultural practices. One of the most captivating aspects of Calabrian heritage is the ancient dance known as the "tarantella." This vibrant dance, with its infectious rhythm and whirlwind movements, embodies the celebratory spirit and unity of the people. Dancing the tarantella at festive gatherings remains a cherished tradition, reflecting the joy and resilience of Calabrians.

Sacred Celebrations: Religious Festivities

Religion plays a vital role in the lives of Calabrians, and religious celebrations are integral to their cultural calendar. Witnessing the elaborate festivities during patron saint celebrations is an awe-inspiring experience. The towns and villages come alive with processions, music, and vibrant displays of faith, illustrating the profound connection between spirituality and community in Calabria.

Passing Down the Legacy: Cultural Preservation

The commitment to preserving their heritage is evident in the efforts of Calabrians to pass down their customs and traditions from one generation to the next. Families and communities take great pride in teaching the younger members about their cultural heritage, ensuring that the ancient arts, crafts, and culinary traditions remain alive and cherished for years to come.

In Calabria, the people's indomitable spirit and strong sense of community stand as a testament to the resilience of the human spirit. Exploring the tapestry of traditions and cultural practices that bind the people of Calabria allows visitors to connect deeply with the region's identity and history, revealing the enduring beauty of a community that has triumphed over challenges, unified in its determination to preserve its heritage, and emerged stronger, forging a future that is firmly rooted in its glorious past.

1.2.2 Hospitality and Generosity: Embracing Strangers as Friends

Hospitality lies at the very heart of Calabrian culture, a cherished value passed down through generations. As you step foot into this enchanting region, you'll immediately feel the embrace of warm smiles and the genuine kindness of its residents. Calabrians take immense pride in their reputation as gracious hosts, and their hospitality extends far beyond mere gestures; it's a heartfelt invitation to experience the true essence of their land and immerse yourself in the joys of their timeless traditions.

Welcoming with Open Arms: The Art of Hospitality

From the moment you arrive in Calabria, you'll be greeted with an overwhelming sense of genuine hospitality. Whether you're a first-time visitor or a returning friend, the people of Calabria have an innate ability to make you feel like you've come home. It's not uncommon to be warmly embraced by locals who eagerly invite you into their homes, eager to share their stories and local delicacies. The art of hospitality is deeply ingrained in their culture, and they take great joy in ensuring that every guest feels like an honored member of their extended family.

An Invitation to Savor: Culinary Delights

Food is an integral part of Calabrian hospitality, and it's a central aspect of any gathering or celebration. Prepare to embark on a gastronomic adventure, where every dish is a labor of love, crafted with the freshest local ingredients and traditional recipes that have been perfected over centuries. Calabrians will delight in presenting you with an array of flavors, from delectable pasta dishes to mouthwatering seafood specialties and robust meats seasoned to perfection. Sharing a meal with new friends in Calabria isn't just about satisfying your hunger; it's about nourishing your soul with the warmth of human connection.

Inviting You into Traditions: A Window into Culture

Hospitality in Calabria goes beyond food and lodging; it's about offering you a glimpse into their time-honored traditions. Whether it's joining in the lively dance of the tarantella during a festive celebration, witnessing the ancient craftsmanship of local artisans, or partaking in religious processions that unite the community, you'll be invited to be a part of the cultural fabric that binds Calabrians together. Sharing in these traditions opens doors to new experiences and deepens your understanding of the region's rich heritage.

Embracing Diversity: A Global Family

Calabrians have a remarkable ability to forge connections with people from all corners of the globe. They welcome travelers from diverse backgrounds and treat them as cherished guests. The culture of hospitality in Calabria transcends borders, making visitors feel valued and embraced, regardless of their origin. In this corner of Southern Italy, you'll find a sense of kinship and belonging that unites people from various walks of life, creating a global family connected by the warmth of Calabrian hospitality.

A Lasting Impression: Memories to Treasure

The memories forged during your time in Calabria will linger long after you depart its shores. The friendships formed, the laughter shared, and the stories exchanged will stay with you as cherished keepsakes of your journey. Calabrians' hospitality leaves a lasting impression, touching the heart and soul of those fortunate enough to experience it. As you bid farewell to this enchanting land, you'll carry with you not just the beauty of its landscapes but also the warmth of its people, forever grateful for the hospitality that made your stay truly unforgettable.

In Calabria, hospitality is more than a custom; it's a way of life – an invitation to embrace the richness of the land, the joy of traditions, and the warmth of human connections. So, allow yourself to be captivated by the open arms and warm hearts of the people of Calabria, and you'll discover that the essence of true hospitality lies in the spirit of making every guest feel at home, sharing the joy of life's simple pleasures, and building bonds that transcend time and distance.

1.2.3 Fiercely Independent Spirit: Nurturing Identity and Pride

Calabrians wear their heritage and identity like a badge of honor, a testament to the resilience of their ancestors and the profound connection they feel to their homeland.

Centuries of historical events and a tapestry of cultural influences have shaped the character of Calabrians, forging a deep sense of belonging that is woven into the very fabric of their lives. To truly understand Calabria, one must embrace the opportunity to engage with its people, listen to their stories, and witness the pride that radiates from within them.

A Cultural Tapestry: Nurturing Identity

Calabria's history is a tapestry woven from the threads of diverse cultures that have left an indelible mark on its people. From the ancient Greeks and Romans to Byzantines, Normans, and beyond, each civilization has contributed to the region's rich heritage. Despite these historical influences, Calabrians have maintained a unique and vibrant identity that distinguishes them from the rest of Italy. Their customs, traditions, and dialect are a testament to their perseverance in preserving the essence of their roots.

A Language of Their Own: The Calabrian Dialect

The Calabrian dialect is a treasure trove of linguistic expressions that have been lovingly passed down through generations. Speaking the Calabrian dialect is an act of cultural preservation, a nod to their past and a celebration of their present. Engaging in conversation with locals in their native tongue opens doors to a deeper connection, allowing you to grasp the nuances of their emotions and the stories they hold dear.

Stories of Strength and Triumph: A Proud Legacy

To know Calabria is to know its people and their stories. They proudly recount tales of the challenges their ancestors faced and the victories they achieved. Stories of resilience during times of adversity, tales of community coming together to overcome hardships, and accounts of triumphs over the odds all form the bedrock of Calabrians' pride. Listening to these stories reveals a people deeply rooted in their past, forging a path to a brighter future.

A Land to Love: Passionate Homeland

Calabrians' love for their homeland is an all-encompassing passion that infuses every aspect of their lives. They draw inspiration from the breathtaking landscapes that surround them, from the azure shores of the coastlines to the snow-capped peaks of the mountains. Their connection to the land is inseparable, and they take great pride in its beauty, diversity, and natural wonders.

Welcoming You with Open Hearts: Sharing Their World

When engaging with Calabrians, you'll be met with genuine enthusiasm as they share their homeland with you. They eagerly welcome visitors, eager to introduce them to the wonders of Calabria. Whether it's inviting you to join in a lively local celebration or guiding you through the charming alleys of their villages, their openness reflects the warmth of their hearts and the sense of joy they find in sharing their beloved region with others.

Embrace the opportunity to immerse yourself in Calabria's vibrant culture and connect with the proud, resilient, and welcoming people who call it home. Listen to their stories, speak their language, and witness the love they have for their heritage and identity. As you delve deeper into the essence of

Calabria, you'll discover a world where pride and belonging intertwine, creating an unbreakable bond between the people and their cherished homeland.

1.3 Language, Customs, and Traditions

The cultural fabric of Calabria is interwoven with a captivating language, customs, and traditions, each contributing to the region's vibrant tapestry of life.

1.3.1 Calabrian Dialect: The Melody of the Land

The Calabrian dialect is a delightful and enchanting reflection of the region's vibrant culture and history. As you embark on your journey through Calabria, you'll discover a language that seems to dance with the rhythms of the land, adding a unique flavor to everyday conversations. Immersing yourself in the local dialect is like unlocking a hidden treasure, as it opens doors to genuine connections and bridges the gap between you and the welcoming locals.

The Music of Words: Echoing the Rhythms of Calabria

When you first hear the Calabrian dialect, you'll be captivated by its melodic cadence and expressive intonation. The locals infuse their speech with passion, and their gestures bring life to their words. Each conversation becomes a symphony of emotions, as the dialect becomes a vessel through which feelings and stories are conveyed.

Unearthing Local Expressions: A Journey into Vernacular

As you delve into the Calabrian dialect, you'll unearth a treasure trove of local expressions and idioms that add color and charm to conversations. From endearing terms of endearment to playful phrases, the dialect offers a glimpse into the heart of Calabrian humor and wit. Learning and using these expressions will undoubtedly elicit smiles and laughter from the locals, as they appreciate your efforts to embrace their language and culture.

Embracing the Dialect: Building Bridges with Locals

The Calabrian dialect is more than just a linguistic tool; it's a key that unlocks the doors to the hearts of the people. As you immerse yourself in their language, you'll find that the locals are delighted to see you making an effort to connect with them on a deeper level. Even simple greetings or expressions of gratitude in the Calabrian dialect can spark joy and create a strong sense of camaraderie.

A Cultural Exchange: Sharing Language and Laughter

Language becomes a bridge that facilitates a genuine cultural exchange. As you learn phrases and engage in conversations with locals, you'll not only be connecting on a linguistic level but also sharing laughter, experiences, and a mutual appreciation for each other's cultures. In this exchange, you'll discover that language is more than just words; it's a pathway to understanding and friendship.

A Lasting Impression: Leaving a Positive Mark

As you journey through Calabria, your willingness to embrace the local dialect will leave a lasting impression on the people you meet. The effort you put into learning a few phrases will be warmly received, and the smiles that widen on their faces will be a testament to the power of language in forging connections.

So, seize the opportunity to dive into the world of the Calabrian dialect. Learn a few phrases, engage in conversations, and let the music of the language carry you deeper into the heart of this enchanting region. As you connect with the locals through their language, you'll experience a sense of belonging and a shared appreciation for the beauty and richness of Calabria's culture.

1.3.2 Customs and Festivals: Celebrating Life's Richness

In Calabria, the passage of time is marked not only by the changing seasons but also by an abundance of vibrant festivals and celebrations that breathe life into the region's cultural tapestry. These events serve as windows into the heart of Calabrian life, offering a glimpse into the customs, traditions, and shared heritage that bind communities together. As a visitor, you have the unique opportunity to immerse yourself in the revelry, taste traditional delicacies, and witness the pageantry that unfolds during these captivating occasions.

A Tapestry of Festivals: Embracing Tradition

Calabria's calendar is adorned with a diverse array of festivals that reflect the region's deep-rooted traditions and historical significance. Each celebration is steeped in meaning and carries with it a sense of pride and belonging for the locals. From ancient folklore events to religious processions, each festival contributes to the vibrant cultural mosaic that defines Calabria.

Religious Devotion: Honoring Patron Saints

Religion holds a special place in the hearts of Calabrians, and religious festivals are celebrated with great fervor and devotion. During these occasions, towns and villages come alive with colorful processions, hymns, and prayers, paying homage to their patron saints. Witnessing the faith and devotion of the people as they carry the statues of saints through the streets is a moving experience, providing a glimpse into the spiritual essence of Calabria.

Seasonal Celebrations: Embracing Nature's Rhythms

Calabria's festivals are often closely intertwined with the changing seasons, celebrating the bountiful gifts that nature bestows upon the land. From the joyous harvest festivals that honor agricultural abundance to the vibrant carnivals that herald the arrival of spring, each event embodies a unique aspect of Calabrian life. You'll find yourself swept up in the excitement as locals come together to celebrate the passing of seasons and the renewal of life.

Timeless Folklore: Keeping Traditions Alive

Ancient folklore events offer a magical window into the region's storied past. Whether it's the lively "Ndocciata" festival in Agnone or the captivating "Ciminata" in Nicotera, these traditions harken back to times long gone. You'll be enchanted by the colorful costumes, evocative music, and mesmerizing performances that bring these age-old customs to life, connecting you with the soulful spirit of Calabria's history.

A Feast for the Senses: Savoring Traditional Delicacies

Food plays an integral role in Calabrian celebrations, and festivals are a feast for the senses. From street vendors offering delectable treats to traditional dishes lovingly prepared in homes and local eateries, you'll have the opportunity to indulge in an array of mouthwatering delicacies. Each bite carries the essence of Calabria's culinary heritage, making these festivals a true delight for food enthusiasts.

Uniting the Community: Vibrant Pageantry

Festivals in Calabria are not just events; they are a reflection of community spirit and solidarity. Families, friends, and neighbors come together to participate in the festivities, forging bonds that strengthen the social fabric of the region. The lively pageantry, spirited dances, and shared laughter create an atmosphere of joy and unity, leaving an enduring impression on those who are fortunate enough to be part of these celebrations.

In Calabria's festivals, you'll discover a profound sense of cultural identity and a genuine connection to the past. Join the revelry, dance to the rhythm of the music, and savor the rich traditions that have been lovingly passed down through generations. As you witness the vibrant pageantry that binds communities together, you'll become an integral part of the cultural mosaic that makes Calabria an enchanting and unforgettable destination.

1.3.3 Artistry and Craftsmanship: The Soul of Handmade Treasures

Calabria is a treasure trove of artisanal craftsmanship, where the hands of skilled artisans breathe life into age-old techniques and create exquisite works of art that embody the essence of the region's cultural heritage. As you wander through the charming towns and villages, you'll encounter a world of craftsmanship that is a testament to the artisans' passion, dedication, and profound connection to their ancestral roots.

Lacework: A Delicate Tradition

Calabria is renowned for its intricate lacework, known as "merletto." This delicate art form has been perfected over centuries, with patterns and designs that reflect the beauty of the region's natural landscapes. Visiting local lace workshops, you'll witness the nimble fingers of artisans skillfully crafting lace pieces that are treasured for their elegance and timeless charm.

Pottery: Shaping Earth's Beauty

The art of pottery in Calabria dates back to ancient times, and the tradition continues to thrive today. Talented potters mold clay into stunning creations that range from functional ceramics to decorative pieces adorned with intricate designs. Each pottery piece captures the essence of Calabria's artistic expression, incorporating motifs inspired by its history and natural surroundings.

Vibrant Textiles: Weaving Colorful Tales

Textiles in Calabria are a vivid expression of the region's identity. Local weavers craft vibrant fabrics and tapestries that showcase the beauty of Calabrian landscapes and cultural symbols. From carpets and tapestries to handwoven garments, these textiles carry the soulful narratives of the artisans and tell stories of their ancestral heritage.

Culinary Artistry: Savoring Tradition

In Calabria, craftsmanship extends to the realm of culinary artistry. The region's renowned delicacies are lovingly prepared using traditional techniques and treasured family recipes. Whether it's the delectable "nduja," a spicy spreadable salami, or the exquisite "fileja" pasta, each dish is a masterpiece that encapsulates the flavors and culinary wisdom of generations.

Markets of Inspiration: A Haven for Craft Lovers

Exploring local markets in Calabria is a sensory delight. Here, you'll find an array of handmade creations displayed with pride. From the bustling open-air markets to the quaint artisanal shops, you can browse through a myriad of unique pieces that bear the mark of each artisan's individuality. Purchasing a handcrafted souvenir not only supports local craftsmanship but also allows you to take a piece of Calabria's artistic heritage home with you.

Passing Down the Torch: A Legacy of Artistry

The tradition of artisanal craftsmanship in Calabria is more than just a livelihood; it's a way of life that is passed down from one generation to the next. Young apprentices learn from experienced masters, absorbing the techniques and the passion that fuel this timeless art. Through this intergenerational exchange, the legacy of Calabria's artistry is safeguarded, ensuring that these invaluable traditions continue to flourish in the modern world.

In Calabria's artisanal craftsmanship, you'll discover a world where creativity and tradition intertwine, creating works of art that resonate with the soul and tell stories of a rich cultural heritage. Embrace the opportunity to explore local workshops and markets, and you'll unveil the heart and soul of Calabria's artisans, who infuse each creation with the beauty, history, and spirit of this enchanting region.

Immerse yourself in the geography, people, and culture of Calabria, and you'll find a world brimming with untold wonders and authentic experiences waiting to be uncovered.

CHAPTER TWO

Top Destinations in Calabria

2.1 Exploring Reggio Calabria: Gateway to the South

Reggio Calabria, often referred to simply as Reggio, is a city that stands as the gateway to the southern region of Italy. Nestled between the Aspromonte Mountains and the pristine waters of the Ionian Sea, Reggio Calabria offers a captivating blend of history, culture, and natural beauty.

2.1.1 Historical Marvels

Reggio Calabria, with its strategic location at the toe of Italy's boot, boasts a captivating historical heritage that dates back to ancient times. Stepping into the city is like taking a journey through the annals of history, where the past intertwines with the present to create an enchanting tapestry of cultural significance.

One of the crown jewels of Reggio Calabria's historical treasures is the National Archaeological Museum of Magna Graecia. Housed within a majestic building, the museum holds an exceptional collection of artifacts that offers insight into the region's rich ancient Greek heritage. Among the most famous exhibits are the Riace Bronzes, two extraordinary sculptures of warriors cast in bronze during the 5th century BC. These lifelike masterpieces have captivated art enthusiasts and scholars for centuries, with their stunning craftsmanship and intriguing stories.

The Riace Bronzes, discovered off the coast of Riace Marina in 1972, stand as a testament to the profound artistry of the ancient Greeks. Their expressive faces and detailed anatomical features demonstrate the pinnacle of ancient sculpting techniques. The museum carefully showcases these priceless sculptures, allowing visitors to marvel at their beauty and appreciate their historical significance.

Apart from the Riace Bronzes, the National Archaeological Museum of Magna Graecia exhibits an array of other fascinating artifacts, including pottery, coins, and architectural elements, providing visitors with a comprehensive understanding of Magna Graecia's cultural and artistic legacy.

Another historical gem within Reggio Calabria is the Roman Baths, a testament to the city's Roman past. The remains of these ancient thermal baths allow visitors to imagine the opulence and grandeur that once graced the city during the Roman era. Strolling through the ruins, visitors can visualize the communal baths, steam rooms, and changing areas that were once bustling with activity and served as a place for relaxation and socializing.

Dominating the city's skyline, the Aragonese Castle is yet another emblematic historical landmark in Reggio Calabria. This medieval fortress has witnessed centuries of tumultuous history and has been an essential part of the city's defense system throughout various epochs. Perched on a hill, the castle provides commanding views of the surrounding landscape and the shimmering waters of the Strait of Messina.

As visitors explore the imposing walls and towers of the Aragonese Castle, they can't help but feel transported back in time, imagining the battles, triumphs, and defeats that have shaped the course of the city's history. Today, the castle stands as a symbol of resilience and a connection to Reggio Calabria's past, reminding all who visit of the city's storied heritage.

2.1.2 Seafront Promenade and Lungomare Falcomatà

Reggio Calabria's allure extends beyond its historical treasures, encompassing the city's breathtaking coastal views and inviting seafront promenade. Lungomare Falcomatà, the city's elegant waterfront promenade, beckons visitors and locals alike to embrace the relaxed pace of life by the sea.

Lined with towering palm trees, Lungomare Falcomatà offers a picturesque setting for leisurely strolls or peaceful moments of reflection. The gentle breeze from the Ionian Sea carries the scent of saltwater and the promise of a tranquil escape from the hustle and bustle of daily life.

As one walks along the promenade, the sparkling blue waters of the Ionian Sea provide a soothing backdrop, creating a serene ambiance that encourages relaxation and contemplation. Visitors can find ample seating areas, perfect for sitting back and basking in the beauty of the surroundings.

Charming cafes and restaurants dot the promenade, providing an ideal setting to savor a cup of freshly brewed coffee or indulge in traditional Calabrian delicacies while taking in the mesmerizing seascape. The sound of laughter and chatter fills the air as locals and visitors mingle, sharing stories and creating lasting memories.

At dusk, the sunsets over the Strait of Messina are a sight to behold. The sky transforms into a palette of warm hues, casting a golden glow upon the city and sea. Couples and families gather along Lungomare Falcomatà to witness this daily spectacle, an enchanting moment of natural beauty that leaves a lasting impression on the heart.

Throughout the year, the promenade comes alive with various events and festivities. From cultural festivals to live music performances, Lungomare Falcomatà becomes a vibrant stage for celebration, uniting the community and welcoming guests with open arms.

For those seeking a more active experience, the promenade offers opportunities for cycling, jogging, and rollerblading, inviting enthusiasts to embark on an invigorating journey along the seafront. The open spaces and well-maintained paths provide a perfect setting for outdoor activities, promoting a healthy lifestyle amidst the inspiring coastal backdrop.

In the evening, Lungomare Falcomatà is a place to embrace the Italian tradition of "passeggiata," a leisurely evening walk with friends and family. The seafront promenade becomes a bustling social hub, radiating warmth and camaraderie as people connect, laughter fills the air, and the sense of community thrives.

Lungomare Falcomatà truly captures the essence of Reggio Calabria - a place where history intertwines with natural beauty, and the rhythm of life is harmoniously attuned to the ebb and flow of the sea.

2.1.3 Traditional Cuisine

Reggio Calabria's culinary scene is a delightful fusion of flavors, where fresh, locally-sourced ingredients and traditional cooking techniques combine to create a feast for the senses. As a city nestled by the sea, Reggio Calabria boasts a rich array of seafood dishes that showcase the region's unique gastronomic heritage.

Calabria's coastal waters teem with an abundance of seafood, ranging from succulent swordfish to tender anchovies and squid. Local fishermen diligently ply their trade, bringing in a daily catch that graces the tables of Reggio Calabria's finest restaurants and humble family kitchens alike.

One of the signature dishes that perfectly captures the essence of Calabrian cuisine is "swordfish alla ghiotta." This mouthwatering preparation sees fresh swordfish cooked to perfection with tomatoes, capers, olives, and a hint of chili pepper. The combination of savory flavors and the delicate texture of the fish makes this dish a favorite among both locals and visitors.

Another classic Calabrian seafood specialty is "baccalà," salted codfish that undergoes a meticulous soaking process to remove the salt before being prepared in various ways. From being sautéed with garlic, cherry tomatoes, and black olives to being cooked in a flavorful stew, baccalà offers a diverse range of delicious options.

Reggio Calabria's culinary wonders aren't limited to seafood alone; the city's traditional dishes also include a delightful selection of pasta creations. "Pasta ca muddica" is a prime example of Calabria's ability to elevate simple ingredients into something extraordinary. This rustic dish features pasta coated with toasted breadcrumbs, anchovies, and chili peppers, resulting in a uniquely satisfying taste that tantalizes the palate.

For those with a taste for something heartier, Calabria's traditional meat dishes offer a delightful array of flavors. "Nduja," a fiery, spreadable salami made from pork and Calabrian chili peppers, is a local delicacy that packs a punch. Whether spread on a slice of rustic bread or incorporated into various recipes, "nduja" showcases the region's passion for bold, robust flavors.

When it comes to sweet indulgences, Reggio Calabria doesn't disappoint. The city's traditional desserts reflect the richness of its cultural heritage. "Pitta 'mpigliata" is a popular pastry that graces the tables during festive occasions. This delightful confection features layers of thin pastry filled with walnuts, almonds, figs, honey, and spices, resulting in a harmonious blend of flavors and textures.

Another sweet treat that captivates the taste buds is "torrone," a scrumptious nougat made with honey, almonds, and citrus zest. As you take a bite of this ancient delicacy, you'll savor the contrasting textures and the delightful balance of sweetness and nuttiness.

Complementing the exquisite flavors of Reggio Calabria's cuisine is the strong sense of community that surrounds food. Mealtime is an opportunity for gathering, storytelling, and sharing laughter with loved ones. Whether enjoying a feast in a bustling trattoria or partaking in a home-cooked meal with locals, the hospitality and warmth of Calabrian culture are ever-present.

Exploring the culinary traditions of Reggio Calabria is a journey that goes beyond the taste buds - it is an immersive experience that allows visitors to connect with the region's soul and understand the profound cultural significance of food in the heart of Italy's best-kept secret.

2.2 Tropea: The Jewel of the Tyrrhenian Coast

Nestled on a rocky cliff overlooking the turquoise waters of the Tyrrhenian Sea, Tropea is a coastal gem renowned for its stunning landscapes and charming atmosphere. This picturesque town has been enticing travelers with its breathtaking views and relaxed vibe.

2.2.1 The Magnificent Tropea Cathedral

Perched dramatically atop a rocky promontory, the Tropea Cathedral stands as a magnificent testament to the town's rich religious heritage and architectural prowess. Dedicated to the Virgin Mary, the cathedral's imposing presence dominates the skyline, drawing both locals and visitors to its awe-inspiring beauty.

As one approaches the Tropea Cathedral, the sheer grandeur of its facade leaves a lasting impression. The intricately carved stone facade showcases a captivating blend of architectural styles, reflecting the cathedral's long history and the influences of various periods. The main entrance, adorned with sculpted religious motifs, invites all to step inside and experience the sanctuary's spiritual embrace.

Venturing through the cathedral's doors reveals an interior that is equally impressive. The soaring nave, adorned with elegant arches and majestic columns, exudes a sense of sacred magnificence. Light filters through stained glass windows, casting a colorful glow upon the marble floors and intricately designed altar.

The cathedral's artistic treasures are a testament to the town's historical significance and the devotion of its people. Marvelous frescoes, painted by skilled artists throughout the centuries, grace the walls and ceilings, recounting biblical stories and scenes from Tropea's religious past. These masterful artworks serve as windows into the region's cultural legacy, preserving moments of devotion and spirituality for generations to come.

The highlight of the Tropea Cathedral is its beautifully preserved Byzantine icon of the Virgin Mary, believed to have been brought to the town in the 11th century. The icon, known as the Madonna of Romania, is a revered symbol of faith and protection for the local community. Pilgrims and worshippers come from far and wide to pay their respects to this sacred icon, seeking blessings and solace in its benevolent presence.

2.2.2 Tropea's Gorgeous Beaches

Nestled along the Tyrrhenian Sea, Tropea boasts a coastline adorned with some of the most breathtaking beaches in Italy. Each beach possesses its own unique charm, offering a diverse range of experiences for travelers seeking relaxation, adventure, or communion with nature.

Praia di Fuoco, a hidden gem accessible only by sea, embodies the essence of an unspoiled paradise. Shielded by towering cliffs, this secluded cove is a haven of tranquility and natural beauty. The pristine waters invite swimmers to indulge in a refreshing dip, while the surrounding cliffs provide adventurous souls with the opportunity to explore hidden caves and grottoes. Praia di Fuoco's secluded ambiance makes it an idyllic spot for those seeking solitude and a connection with nature's serenity.

In contrast, Tropea Beach, with its expanse of fine golden sand, draws sun-seekers and beach enthusiasts from all corners of the world. Framed by turquoise waters that gently kiss the shoreline, this beach is an inviting playground for those who revel in the sun's warm embrace. Beachgoers can bask in the Mediterranean sun, build sandcastles, or simply stroll along the shore, their feet caressed by the gentle lapping of the waves.

Water sports enthusiasts find their haven in Tropea's coastal waters. Snorkeling and scuba diving opportunities abound, allowing visitors to explore the thriving underwater world teeming with vibrant marine life and colorful coral reefs. Windsurfing and sailing also attract adventure seekers, who delight in the sea's playful embrace and the thrill of riding its waves.

2.2.3 Red Onions and Local Delicacies

Beyond its natural beauty, Tropea is renowned for its culinary delights, and at the heart of its gastronomic offerings lies the famous "cipolla di Tropea," or Tropea red onion. These sweet and succulent onions, cultivated in the region's fertile volcanic soil, are a culinary treasure that has earned the town a place of honor in the world of Italian cuisine.

A visit to Tropea's bustling local markets presents a delightful opportunity to savor the flavors of the region. The vibrant displays of Tropea red onions capture the eye and the imagination, showcasing the versatility of this beloved ingredient. From raw slices served in fresh salads to savory onion jams, the Tropea red onion adds a unique sweetness and depth of flavor to a myriad of dishes.

One of the most beloved traditional dishes that celebrates the Tropea red onion is "caponata di cipolla di Tropea," a flavorful relish made by slow-cooking the onions with a medley of aromatic herbs and spices. This delicious condiment pairs perfectly with grilled meats, cheeses, and crusty bread, offering a delightful explosion of tastes and textures.

While exploring Tropea's culinary landscape, travelers shouldn't miss the opportunity to indulge in another local specialty: "fileja" pasta. This traditional hand-rolled pasta is skillfully crafted using a knitting needle-like tool, resulting in a unique texture that captures the sauce it accompanies.

The pairing of "fileja" pasta with "ragù," a hearty meat-based sauce slow-cooked with tomatoes and aromatic herbs, creates a gastronomic symphony that exemplifies the artistry of Calabrian cuisine. The flavors meld harmoniously, inviting diners to savor every mouthful and appreciate the dedication that goes into each dish.

As the sun sets over the Tyrrhenian Sea, Tropea's culinary wonders come alive in the town's charming trattorias and quaint restaurants. With each bite, visitors are immersed in a culinary journey that unites the bounty of the land and sea, the warmth of local hospitality, and the rich cultural heritage that defines Tropea's soulful cuisine.

A visit to Tropea becomes a celebration of the senses, where the majestic Tropea Cathedral, the sun-kissed beaches, and the flavors of the Tropea red onion create an experience that lingers in the heart and beckons travelers to return to Italy's cherished jewel on the Tyrrhenian Coast.

2.3 Cosenza: Where History Meets Nature

Nestled amidst rugged mountains and fertile valleys, Cosenza is a city that seamlessly blends its historical heritage with the surrounding natural beauty. As one of Calabria's oldest cities, Cosenza presents a captivating mix of ancient ruins, medieval architecture, and scenic landscapes.

2.3.1 The Swabian Castle and Historic Center

Perched majestically on a hill overlooking the city, the Swabian Castle stands as an iconic symbol of Cosenza's storied past and enduring legacy. Built during the Norman period, this medieval fortress has witnessed centuries of history unfold within its ancient walls. Today, it welcomes visitors to explore its fascinating heritage and offers panoramic views that showcase the beauty of Cosenza and the surrounding Crati River Valley.

As visitors ascend the hill towards the Swabian Castle, they are greeted with breathtaking vistas that stretch across the city and beyond. The strategic location of the castle allowed it to control important trade routes and act as a defensive stronghold during tumultuous times. The robust walls and watchtowers evoke a sense of grandeur and resilience, reminding all who visit of the castle's historic significance.

Stepping inside the Swabian Castle is like stepping back in time. The well-preserved interior features a maze of chambers, halls, and courtyards that tell tales of knights, nobles, and rulers who once walked these very grounds. Explore the castle's impressive towers, such as the Torre San Matteo and Torre Bragantina, which offer panoramic views of Cosenza's modern urban landscape and the picturesque countryside.

Adjacent to the castle lies the enchanting historic center of Cosenza, a place where time seems to stand still. The medieval alleys and cobblestone streets wind their way through the heart of the city, leading visitors on a captivating journey through centuries of history. Imposing palaces and charming buildings bear witness to Cosenza's illustrious past, and each step reveals hidden gems waiting to be discovered.

The Piazza XV Marzo, the main square of the historic center, serves as a lively gathering place where locals and tourists congregate. Cafes and trattorias spill out onto the square, filling the air with the enticing aroma of freshly brewed coffee and delectable dishes. The lively chatter of conversations intermingles with the sounds of street musicians, creating a vibrant ambiance that is uniquely Cosenza.

Immerse yourself in the bustling atmosphere of the local markets, where vendors proudly display their wares, showcasing the region's artisanal craftsmanship and culinary delights. Here, you can find handmade ceramics, intricate lacework, and traditional Calabrian products that make for perfect souvenirs to cherish the memories of your journey through Cosenza.

2.3.2 The Sila National Park

Beyond the city's historical wonders, Cosenza beckons nature enthusiasts to venture into the pristine wilderness of the Sila National Park. A short distance from the urban bustle, the park's vast expanse of verdant forests, serene lakes, and breathtaking landscapes await those seeking an unforgettable outdoor adventure.

The Sila National Park, often referred to as "La Sila," is a protected natural paradise that spans over 700 square kilometers. Its ancient forests of beech, fir, and pine trees are a sanctuary for wildlife, providing a habitat for rare and endangered species. Birdwatchers can delight in the diverse avian population, including majestic birds of prey and vibrant migratory species.

Hiking through the lush trails of La Sila is a transformative experience. The quietude of nature envelops you as you meander through dense woodlands, where rays of sunlight filter through the canopy, creating a mesmerizing play of shadows on the forest floor. For those who seek more challenging treks, the park offers rugged paths that lead to stunning viewpoints, rewarding hikers with panoramic vistas that stretch as far as the eye can see.

As you explore deeper into the heart of La Sila, you'll encounter the park's serene lakes, such as Lake Cecita and Lake Arvo. These mirror-like bodies of water reflect the surrounding mountainous landscape, evoking a sense of tranquility and serenity. Here, you can enjoy leisurely boat rides or simply sit by the lakeshores, allowing the beauty of the scenery to rejuvenate your spirit.

During the winter months, La Sila transforms into a winter wonderland, offering opportunities for skiing and snowboarding. The pristine slopes attract both seasoned skiers and beginners, inviting them to glide through the powdery snow and revel in the joys of winter sports amidst the stunning backdrop of the park's snow-capped peaks.

Throughout the year, the Sila National Park invites visitors to immerse themselves in the rhythms of nature and discover the true essence of Calabria's untamed beauty. Whether hiking through ancient forests, observing wildlife in its natural habitat, or simply relishing the peace and serenity of the wilderness, La Sila offers an authentic and unforgettable connection with the natural world.

2.3.3 Gastronomy and Local Flavors

Cosenza's culinary scene is a celebration of the region's traditions and flavors, embracing the bounty of the land and the expertise of local artisans. The city's gastronomy is a true reflection of Calabria's rich cultural heritage, where time-honored recipes and locally sourced ingredients take center stage.

A visit to Cosenza's lively markets reveals a vibrant array of traditional Calabrian products. Cured meats, such as "soppressata" and "capocollo," are delicately seasoned and aged to perfection, boasting robust flavors that pay homage to age-old curing techniques. These savory delights make for the perfect accompaniment to regional cheeses, such as "pecorino" and "caciocavallo," each with its own distinctive character and taste.

Artisanal bread, a staple of Calabrian cuisine, is lovingly prepared by local bakers, who take pride in preserving ancient baking traditions. From the classic "pane di grano duro" to the delightful "pane di cipolla," an onion-flavored bread, each variety reflects the dedication and skill that goes into every loaf.

As a city that cherishes its traditions and religious customs, Cosenza holds special significance during Easter, when locals indulge in the beloved sweet bread known as "cuzzupa." Families and friends come together to bake and share these elaborately decorated loaves, passing down cherished recipes from generation to generation. The preparation of "cuzzupa" is a labor of love, and each batch is uniquely shaped and adorned with colored eggs, symbolizing the season of rebirth and renewal.

The culinary journey continues with "pasta e fagioli," a hearty dish that epitomizes the simplicity and soulfulness of Calabrian home cooking. This pasta and bean soup, enriched with tomatoes, herbs, and a hint of chili pepper, provides comforting nourishment that warms the heart and soul.

No visit to Cosenza would be complete without sampling "sagne chine," an ancient type of pasta crafted by skilled artisans. These thin, hand-rolled strips of pasta are a true labor of love, made from a simple dough of flour and water and shaped using a unique knitting-needle-like tool called "chine." The result is a delightfully chewy and satisfying pasta that pairs wonderfully with a variety of sauces, from rich meat ragù to flavorful seafood creations.

Cosenza's culinary delights extend to its dessert offerings, where traditional sweets add a touch of sweetness to life's simplest moments. Indulge in "calzoncelli," irresistible pastry pockets filled with honey, nuts, and spices, or savor the aroma of "amaretti," almond-flavored macaroons that melt in your mouth.

The city's trattorias and family-run restaurants offer a genuine taste of Calabria's soulful cuisine, where the warmth of local hospitality complements the richness of flavors. Each dish is a testament to the region's identity, culture, and love for culinary heritage, inviting you to savor the essence of Cosenza with every delicious bite.

In the heart of Cosenza, the Swabian Castle and its historic center stand as a testament to the city's enduring spirit and vibrant cultural heritage. As visitors explore these ancient landmarks, they gain a deeper understanding of Cosenza's storied past, and its people's indomitable pride in preserving their traditions.

Beyond the city's historic allure, Cosenza also serves as a gateway to the untamed beauty of the Sila National Park. Nature enthusiasts and adventure seekers are drawn to this pristine wilderness, where the enchanting landscapes and diverse wildlife offer a captivating outdoor experience.

The city's gastronomy is a delightful journey that captivates the senses, featuring a cornucopia of flavors that reflect the region's traditions and culinary expertise. From cured meats and artisanal bread to traditional sweets and soul-warming dishes, Cosenza's culinary offerings are a tribute to the rich cultural tapestry that defines this captivating destination.

As you wander through the medieval alleys of the historic center, bask in the breathtaking views from the Swabian Castle, and immerse yourself in the tranquility of the Sila National Park, you'll find that Cosenza offers a harmonious blend of history, nature, and gastronomy - an all-encompassing experience that leaves an indelible mark on your soul and beckons you to return to this enchanting corner of Calabria.

2.4 Catanzaro: A City Between Mountains and Sea

Catanzaro, the capital of Calabria, is perched on the Calabrian hills, affording visitors breathtaking vistas of both the Ionian Sea and the Apennine Mountains. With its mix of ancient ruins and modern amenities, Catanzaro offers a unique experience.

2.4.1 Catanzaro's Historical Treasures

Catanzaro, with its ancient roots dating back to the Roman era, is a city steeped in history and dotted with fascinating remnants of its past. As visitors meander through its streets, they will discover the vestiges of a bygone era, each telling a tale of the city's enduring resilience and cultural heritage.

At the heart of Catanzaro stands the impressive Castello Normanno, a medieval fortress that bears witness to the city's strategic importance throughout the ages. Perched high on a hill, this imposing structure offers commanding views of the Calabrian countryside, stretching as far as the Ionian Sea and the Tyrrhenian Sea. As visitors climb the fortress's ancient walls and explore its historic chambers, they'll be transported back in time, imagining the knights, lords, and noblewomen who once called this castle home.

Continuing their journey through time, visitors will encounter the Cathedral of Santa Maria Assunta, a masterpiece of Calabrian Baroque architecture. The cathedral's facade, adorned with ornate carvings and intricate stonework, showcases the skill and artistry of local craftsmen. Inside, the cathedral's awe-inspiring interiors, embellished with sumptuous frescoes and elaborate altars, exude a sense of divine beauty and tranquility. As visitors gaze upon the ornate ceiling and magnificent artwork, they'll find themselves immersed in the spiritual aura that has drawn the faithful for generations.

2.4.2 The Natural Beauty of La Sila

Beyond the city's historical allure, Catanzaro serves as a gateway to the breathtaking La Sila plateau, a realm of untouched wilderness and natural splendor. Nature lovers and outdoor enthusiasts alike will be enchanted by the boundless beauty that unfolds before them.

La Sila, often referred to as "The Green Heart of Calabria," is a vast mountainous region that enchants visitors with its dense forests, pristine lakes, and undulating landscapes. Hiking trails crisscross the plateau, leading adventurers through forests of centuries-old trees, where the scent of pine fills the air and sunlight filters through the foliage, creating a mesmerizing play of shadows on the forest floor.

During the winter months, La Sila transforms into a snowy wonderland, beckoning skiers and snowboarders to its slopes. As travelers glide down the powdery trails, they are treated to panoramic views of the snow-capped peaks and the enchanting silence of the winter wilderness.

For those seeking tranquility, La Sila's serene lakes, such as Lake Ampollino and Lake Arvo, offer a tranquil respite amidst the surrounding mountains. The crystal-clear waters mirror the surrounding landscape, creating a breathtaking scene that invites visitors to pause and savor the beauty of nature's reflection.

2.4.3 Local Art and Craftsmanship

Catanzaro's artistic heritage is a testament to the city's enduring tradition of craftsmanship. Wander through the city's charming streets, and you'll encounter the works of local artisans that reflect the soul of Calabria's cultural identity.

In artisan workshops, skilled craftsmen meticulously shape clay into delicate pottery pieces adorned with intricate patterns and vibrant colors. Each piece bears the mark of the artisan's passion for their craft, and visitors can take home these unique creations as souvenirs that embody the spirit of Catanzaro.

Woodwork is another cherished art form in Catanzaro, with local artisans carving exquisite sculptures and intricate designs that reflect the region's natural beauty and cultural heritage. The skillful hands of these craftsmen transform pieces of wood into works of art, capturing the essence of Calabria's soulful traditions.

Lacework, known as "merletto," is a renowned craft in Catanzaro, and the delicate lace creations have adorned elegant garments and decorative items for centuries. The city's lace artisans meticulously weave intricate patterns with fine threads, carrying on a tradition that has been passed down through generations.

As readers explore the pages of "Calabria Escapades: Exploring Italy's Best-Kept Secret," they will be captivated by the allure of Catanzaro's historical treasures, immersed in the serenity of La Sila's natural beauty, and enchanted by the artistry and craftsmanship that define the city's cultural heritage. This travel guide is an invitation to embark on a transformative journey through Calabria, where hidden wonders, timeless traditions, and unforgettable experiences await at every turn. Whether it's traversing ancient fortresses, embracing the wilderness, or savoring the artistic essence of Catanzaro, this book promises to be a portal to the heart and soul of Italy's best-kept secret.

CHAPTER THREE

Natural Wonders of Calabria

3.1 Sila National Park: A Wilderness Retreat

Nestled amidst the rugged terrain of Calabria, Sila National Park stands as a pristine and enchanting wilderness retreat for nature enthusiasts and adventure seekers alike. Spanning an expansive 740 square miles (1,917 square kilometers), this breathtaking natural wonder is a picturesque amalgamation of dense forests, meandering rivers, and serene alpine lakes. The park's three high plateaus—Sila Grande, Sila Greca, and Sila Piccola—offer a landscape that is as diverse as it is captivating, inviting travelers to immerse themselves in the region's untamed beauty and tranquil charm.

Exploring Sila Grande, visitors are immediately enveloped in a realm of beech, fir, and majestic pine trees that seem to reach for the skies. These ancient forests, teeming with life, serve as a refuge for a variety of wildlife, including graceful deer, elusive wild boars, and the rare and enigmatic Calabrian wolf. As sunlight filters through the canopy, the forest floor becomes a canvas of dappled light, making it an ideal habitat for a myriad of bird species, a paradise for birdwatchers and nature enthusiasts alike.

Traversing the network of hiking trails that crisscross this woodland wonderland, adventurers are treated to a symphony of sounds—the melodious chorus of songbirds, the whispering of leaves in the breeze, and the gentle gurgling of hidden streams. The trails lead to scenic viewpoints that offer awe-inspiring vistas of the undulating landscape, stretching far beyond the horizon. Whether it's a leisurely stroll or a challenging hike, each step in Sila Grande is an opportunity to forge a deeper connection with the natural world and find solace in its untouched splendor.

In contrast to Sila Grande's towering forests, Sila Greca presents a more tranquil and pastoral setting. Rolling hills adorned with olive groves, vineyards, and fruit orchards dominate the countryside, creating a bucolic charm that harkens back to a simpler time. The landscape is dotted with quaint villages, each with its own unique character and history, where time-honored traditions and warm hospitality welcome curious travelers.

Within these picturesque hamlets, the essence of the rustic Calabrian way of life is palpable. Visitors have the opportunity to engage with the locals, who take great pride in preserving their heritage. The cuisine here is an irresistible invitation to indulge in authentic flavors, as traditional recipes are passed down through generations. Whether it's savoring the richness of homemade pasta dishes, tasting the distinct flavors of locally produced cheese, or relishing the sweetness of sun-ripened fruits, each culinary experience is a celebration of the region's cultural identity.

For those yearning for an alpine escape, Sila Piccola presents an idyllic setting with its crystal-clear lakes and rugged peaks. This alpine wonderland, with its cool and invigorating air, offers an ideal refuge during the warmer months. Here, pristine lakes mirror the surrounding landscape, creating breathtaking reflections that stir the soul. Fishing enthusiasts can try their luck in the clear waters, seeking the prized trout that inhabit these mountain streams.

As the seasons change and winter casts its snowy blanket over the land, Sila Piccola transforms into a magical wonderland—a paradise for winter sports enthusiasts. Snow-capped peaks invite skiers and snowboarders to glide down powdery slopes, while snowshoeing and cross-country skiing trails cater to those seeking a more serene and contemplative winter experience. Families can enjoy ice-skating on frozen lakes, creating cherished memories against the backdrop of a winter wonderland.

Throughout the year, Sila National Park is a playground for outdoor enthusiasts, offering a diverse array of activities to suit every taste and interest. From the tranquil pleasures of birdwatching and nature walks to the adrenaline-pumping excitement of winter sports and challenging hikes, the park caters to individuals seeking both solitude and adventure. With its pristine landscapes and unspoiled charm, Sila National Park embodies the soul of Calabria, a land where nature reigns supreme, inviting visitors to embark on a journey of discovery, self-reflection, and boundless wonder.

3.2 Aspromonte National Park: Where Landscapes Inspire

Aspromonte National Park beckons adventurers to explore its untamed beauty—a landscape that has inspired artists, poets, and dreamers for centuries. Encompassing the southernmost tip of the Apennine Mountains, this rugged terrain is a testament to the unyielding forces of nature. This captivating wilderness, with its soaring peaks and deep valleys, is a sanctuary of biodiversity and cultural heritage, inviting travelers to embark on a journey of discovery and connection with the essence of Calabria's soul.

The park's centerpiece is Mount Consolino, a majestic peak towering at 1,956 meters above sea level. From its summit, a breathtaking panorama of the surrounding valleys and the shimmering Ionian Sea unfolds before the eyes of intrepid trekkers. To reach this pinnacle, adventurers must traverse challenging hiking trails that wind through rocky terrains, lush forests, and cascading waterfalls. Each step taken on this ascent brings a profound sense of achievement, and as they reach the summit, a feeling of oneness with the natural world envelops them.

Throughout Aspromonte, diverse ecosystems weave a tapestry of life, sheltering a rich array of flora and fauna. Ancient beech and oak forests, with trees that have stood for centuries, provide a sanctuary for rare and endangered species. Among these ancient giants, elusive creatures like the golden eagle and peregrine falcon soar majestically, adding to the park's allure as a paradise for birdwatchers and wildlife enthusiasts.

As the seasons change, the landscape of Aspromonte transforms, each presenting its own unique beauty. In spring, wildflowers carpet the meadows with a vibrant array of colors, and migratory birds make their graceful return, filling the air with melodious songs. Summer brings a symphony of life, as the forests hum with the buzz of insects, and the gentle rustling of leaves harmonizes with the gentle flow of mountain streams. Autumn arrives with a breathtaking display of golden hues, as the leaves of deciduous trees paint the landscape with warm and fiery tones. Even in winter, Aspromonte dons a snowy coat, transforming into a glistening winter wonderland, offering a serene and tranquil escape for those seeking solace in the embrace of nature.

Beyond its natural splendor, Aspromonte proudly embraces a rich cultural heritage that bears witness to its historical significance. Amongst the peaks and valleys, the remnants of ancient civilizations can still be found, evoking tales of a bygone era. Greek and Roman ruins stand as silent testaments to the passage of time, igniting the imaginations of visitors and conjuring images of ancient civilizations that once thrived in these lands. These archaeological treasures not only impart knowledge of the past but also add depth and context to the modern-day identity of Calabria.

As visitors venture deeper into Aspromonte's heart, they become immersed in a world of folklore and legends, handed down through generations. Stories of mythical creatures, heroic deeds, and enduring traditions infuse the landscape with a sense of mystique and wonder. Local communities hold these tales close to their hearts, keeping the flame of their cultural heritage alive, and sharing them with visitors who come to listen and learn. It is in these moments of storytelling and connection that travelers truly understand the essence of Aspromonte—a land of magic and mystery, where the lines between reality and myth blur.

To truly experience Aspromonte is to partake in the rhythm of the land, to listen to the whispers of the trees, and to marvel at the vastness of the starlit skies above. It is to feel the heartbeat of Calabria and understand the profound relationship that its people share with the natural world. Each step taken through its untamed beauty is a step closer to unlocking the secrets of the past and embracing the soul of the present.

Throughout the seasons, the park hosts a myriad of events and festivals, celebrating the unique cultural heritage of the region. Festive gatherings are vibrant with music, dance, and culinary delights, as locals come together to share the essence of their identity with the world. These celebrations are a testimony to the resilience of a people who have cherished their land for centuries, and who continue to preserve its treasures for generations to come.

In the embrace of Aspromonte's wilderness, travelers find themselves transformed. The journey through its rugged terrain becomes a pilgrimage of self-discovery, fostering a deep sense of respect and reverence for the natural world. As they bid farewell to this land of inspiration, they carry with them not only memories of breathtaking landscapes and ancient ruins but also an indelible connection to the heart and soul of Calabria.

3.3 The Ionian Coast: Sun, Sand, and Serenity

Stretching along the eastern shoreline of Calabria, the Ionian Coast unveils a sun-drenched paradise where the azure waters of the Ionian Sea caress sandy beaches and picturesque cliffs. This coastal stretch, known for its warm Mediterranean climate, invites travelers to indulge in moments of relaxation and serenity, where time slows down, and the worries of the world seem to fade away.

As the sun rises over the horizon, the Ionian Coast awakens with a golden glow, setting the stage for another day of blissful beach adventures and unforgettable experiences. The coastline unfolds like a treasure trove of natural wonders, each destination offering a unique charm and allure that beckons travelers to explore and discover the hidden gems scattered along the shore.

One of the crown jewels of the Ionian Coast is Tropea, a coastal gem often referred to as the "Jewel of the Tyrrhenian Sea." Perched on a dramatic cliff overlooking the sea, Tropea exudes a magnetic charm, drawing visitors from far and wide. The iconic sight of the Santa Maria dell'Isola sanctuary, perched atop a rocky outcrop, captures the imagination and provides a breathtaking backdrop for lazy beach days and unforgettable sunsets. Strolling through the narrow streets of the historic center, travelers find themselves transported back in time, where the echoes of history resonate in every cobblestone and medieval building.

A short distance southward lies Capo Vaticano, a natural reserve that showcases some of the most pristine white beaches and crystal-clear waters in the region. Here, the sea teems with marine life, making it a paradise for snorkeling and diving enthusiasts. Underneath the surface, a vibrant underwater world comes to life, with colorful corals swaying gently in the currents, and schools of tropical fish darting playfully through the turquoise waters. Exploring this underwater realm is like stepping into a living aquarium, where each stroke of the fin reveals new marvels of nature's design.

Beyond the allure of the beaches, the Ionian Coast offers a captivating blend of coastal towns and villages, where visitors can immerse themselves in the authentic local life and culture. Open-air markets burst with a kaleidoscope of colors, as vendors proudly display their fresh produce, handcrafted goods, and local specialties. The scent of freshly caught seafood wafts through the air, tempting passersby with the promise of a mouthwatering culinary experience. Friendly locals welcome visitors with warm smiles, eager to share stories of their heritage and traditions, creating an atmosphere of genuine hospitality that leaves a lasting impression.

In the heart of the Ionian Coast lies Catanzaro, the regional capital, perched dramatically on a hillside overlooking the Ionian Sea. As travelers ascend the winding roads to the city's historic center, they are rewarded with panoramic views that stretch far and wide. The city's rich history is evident in its architecture, where centuries-old churches and palaces stand as witnesses to the passage of time. Catanzaro is also known for its vibrant cultural scene, with theaters, galleries, and museums that showcase the region's artistic legacy.

Further south, Reggio Calabria awaits with its captivating blend of history and natural beauty. The seafront promenade, known as the "Lungomare," offers a scenic walk along the sea, with stunning views of Sicily just across the water. The city's crown jewel is the National Archaeological Museum, renowned for housing the Riace Bronzes, two majestic statues of ancient warriors that have become iconic symbols of Calabria's ancient heritage.

For those seeking a tranquil escape, the coastal town of Roccella Ionica offers a serene retreat where time seems to stand still. Its medieval castle, overlooking the sea, adds an air of mystery and romance to this coastal haven. The town's relaxed atmosphere and pristine beaches make it an ideal destination for unwinding and embracing the unhurried pace of life.

Further down the coastline, Siderno welcomes visitors with its charming old town and inviting beaches. With its roots dating back to antiquity, Siderno invites travelers to wander through its ancient streets, discovering hidden courtyards and quaint squares. A visit to the Church of Santa Maria della Scala reveals stunning Byzantine frescoes, a testament to the region's cultural richness.

As the day turns to dusk, the Ionian Coast transforms into a magical realm of colors, as the setting sun paints the sky with hues of pink, orange, and gold. Locals and travelers alike gather along the shore, drawn together by the allure of the evening spectacle. The sun's descent below the horizon is met with applause and awe, a ritual celebration of nature's beauty and a reminder of the profound connection between humans and the elements.

The allure of the Ionian Coast extends beyond its daytime splendor, as the night brings its own enchantment. Lively seaside bars and restaurants come to life, offering a vibrant ambiance where the clinking of glasses and laughter fill the air. Freshly caught seafood, locally produced wines, and traditional dishes form a culinary symphony that tantalizes the senses. The coastal towns and villages become stages for outdoor performances and concerts, where music and dance become the heartbeat of the night.

Throughout the year, the Ionian Coast hosts a myriad of festivals and events that celebrate its cultural heritage and natural wonders. Local traditions come alive through processions, parades, and folk performances, providing visitors with an opportunity to immerse themselves in the rich tapestry of Calabrian traditions. These vibrant celebrations reflect the warmth and vitality of the region's people, inviting travelers to be part of the festivities and create lasting memories.

The Ionian Coast is not merely a destination; it is an experience that awakens the senses and touches the soul. It is a place where travelers can bask in the warmth of the Mediterranean sun, where the gentle lapping of waves lulls them into a state of tranquility, and where the authentic charm of coastal life leaves an indelible mark on their hearts. It is a haven where time becomes fluid, and the worries of everyday life fade into the background, replaced by a profound sense of connection with nature and the vibrant culture of Calabria.

As the journey along the Ionian Coast draws to a close, travelers depart with a newfound appreciation for the beauty of simplicity and the richness of genuine human connections. The memories of sun-kissed days spent on pristine beaches, of shared laughter and stories exchanged with locals, and of breathtaking sunsets over the glistening sea become cherished souvenirs that endure long after they have left this coastal paradise.

The Ionian Coast remains a sun-drenched sanctuary, where travelers continue to seek moments of serenity and wonder. Its timeless allure calls to adventurers, artists, and dreamers, inviting them to embark on a journey of exploration and self-discovery. In this sun-drenched paradise, where the azure waters caress the shore and the coast embraces the rhythm of life, the Ionian Coast invites all who venture here to leave behind the ordinary and embrace the extraordinary. It is a place where memories are made, and the spirit of Calabria's coastal charm lives on forever.

3.4 The Tyrrhenian Coast: Beaches and Beyond

On the western side of Calabria lies the Tyrrhenian Coast, a captivating stretch that invites travelers to embrace the Mediterranean dream. From quaint fishing villages to lively seaside towns, this coast offers a diverse range of experiences that embody the essence of Italian coastal living—where sun-soaked days, delightful cuisine, and rich cultural heritage come together to create an unforgettable journey.

One of the first treasures encountered along the Tyrrhenian Coast is the charming coastal town of Pizzo Calabro. Renowned for its delicious Tartufo, a unique ice cream dessert that has become a local specialty, Pizzo offers a delightful indulgence for the senses. The narrow cobbled streets of the town wind their way through picturesque squares, revealing glimpses of the sea at every turn. Pizzo's historic heart lies atop a hill, where the imposing Aragonese

Castle perches majestically, offering panoramic views of the azure waters below. As the sun sets over the Tyrrhenian Sea, the town comes alive with an enchanting ambiance, drawing locals and visitors alike to the lively piazzas and the charming waterfront promenade.

Continuing along the coast, the town of Zambrone emerges as an idyllic escape for sunseekers and water sports enthusiasts. The long stretches of sandy beaches are caressed by crystal-clear waters, creating a postcard-perfect setting for relaxation and rejuvenation. Zambrone's coastline is adorned with hidden coves and limestone cliffs, enticing travelers to explore secluded spots and embrace the serenity of nature. From sunbathing on pristine beaches to snorkeling and paddleboarding in the gentle waves, the possibilities for coastal enjoyment are endless.

As the journey continues, the town of Tropea beckons travelers with its ancient roots and architectural wonders. Perched dramatically atop a cliff overlooking the sea, Tropea exudes an aura of timeless elegance. The imposing Norman cathedral stands as a testament to the town's historical and religious significance, while the historic buildings blend harmoniously with the vibrant atmosphere of the bustling streets below. Tropea's rich history is interwoven with tales of conquest, maritime trade, and cultural exchange, making it a captivating destination for history enthusiasts and curious wanderers alike.

Venturing beyond the coastal embrace, the Tyrrhenian Coast's hinterland reveals a hidden world of rolling hills and fertile plains. Here, verdant landscapes are adorned with vineyards and olive groves that produce some of Calabria's finest wines and olive oils. Embarking on a gastronomic journey in this fertile region is a culinary delight, as travelers savor the authentic flavors of the land. The rustic charm of agriturismos beckons visitors to taste local produce, indulge in farm-to-table delicacies, and enjoy the warm hospitality of the local communities. Each meal becomes an opportunity to savor the richness of Calabrian traditions and appreciate the connection between the land and the culture that has thrived for centuries.

Throughout the Tyrrhenian Coast, an abundance of cultural experiences awaits. Festivals celebrating local traditions and religious events bring communities together, and visitors are welcomed to partake in the festivities. The sound of traditional music fills the air, while vibrant processions and colorful parades add an extra layer of excitement and vibrancy to the coastal towns. Time-honored customs are proudly preserved, and ancient rituals continue to shape the cultural identity of the region. Travelers are encouraged to immerse themselves in this living tapestry of tradition, experiencing the heartfelt joy of celebration and the warmth of community spirit.

Exploring the Tyrrhenian Coast is a multifaceted journey that weaves together history, nature, and gastronomy, creating a harmonious symphony of experiences that resonate with the soul. It is a chance to slow down and embrace the simple pleasures of life, where the sun-drenched days unfold at a leisurely pace, and moments of serenity and joy are cherished. Whether it's basking in the sun on sandy beaches, exploring ancient ruins steeped in history, or savoring the delightful flavors of local delicacies, the

Tyrrhenian Coast offers a balanced blend of relaxation and cultural exploration for every traveler.

As the journey along the Tyrrhenian Coast comes to an end, travelers depart with cherished memories and a profound appreciation for the beauty of this coastal paradise. The azure waters, the vibrant sunsets, and the warm embrace of the local culture leave an indelible mark on the heart, calling visitors back to relive the magic of the Mediterranean dream. The Tyrrhenian Coast becomes more than just a destination; it becomes a cherished part of the traveler's story—a place where experiences and emotions merge, creating an everlasting bond with the heart and soul of Calabria's western coastline.

CHAPTER FOUR

Historical Treasures

4.1 Ancient Origins: Magna Graecia and Its Legacy

The region of Calabria, located in the southernmost part of Italy, has a history that stretches back to ancient times. Once known as Magna Graecia, Calabria was a melting pot of cultures and civilizations, making it a unique and fascinating destination for history enthusiasts and travelers alike. In this chapter, we will embark on a captivating journey through the ancient origins of Calabria, exploring the profound influence of the Greek colonists who settled here around the 8th century BC. We will uncover the remnants of once-thriving Greek cities, delve into the myths and legends, and understand the lasting impact of the Greek civilization on Calabria's culture, architecture, and way of life.

The Greek Colonization of Calabria

The story of Magna Graecia began with the arrival of Greek colonists on the shores of present-day Calabria. Drawn by the fertile lands, mild climate, and strategic location, the Greeks established numerous colonies along the Calabrian coast, leaving an indelible mark on the region. These colonies were autonomous city-states that retained close ties with their mother cities in Greece. Sybaris, Croton, and Locri were among the most influential and prosperous Greek cities that once dotted the Calabrian landscape.

Sybaris: The City of Excess

Sybaris, founded in the 8th century BC, was renowned for its wealth and luxury. It was said to be a city of excess, where its inhabitants indulged in the finest food, wine, and entertainment. The term "sybaritic" originated from the reputation of the Sybarites for their extravagant and pleasure-seeking lifestyle. However, this opulence also led to the envy and eventual destruction of the city by the neighboring Croton in 510 BC.

Croton: Birthplace of Pythagoras

In contrast to Sybaris, Croton was known for its disciplined and athletic way of life. It was in this city that the renowned mathematician and philosopher Pythagoras established his school, teaching his famous theorem and influential philosophical ideas. Croton's athletes were celebrated for their victories in the ancient Olympic Games, and the city became a prominent cultural and intellectual center.

Locri: A Center of Culture and Law

Locri, founded by the Locrians from Greece, thrived as a center of culture, art, and law. The Locrians developed a legal system that was influential in the ancient world, and their laws were admired for their fairness and practicality. The city also produced prominent poets and philosophers, contributing significantly to the intellectual landscape of Magna Graecia.

The Influence of Greek Civilization on Calabria

The Greek colonization profoundly influenced Calabria's culture, shaping its identity in significant ways that still resonate today. The Greek language, customs, and traditions found a permanent place in the region, enriching the local heritage. Calabrian dialects still bear traces of ancient Greek, and traditional festivities often reflect ancient Greek rituals and beliefs.

Architecture and Urban Planning

The Greek colonists brought with them their architectural knowledge and expertise, giving rise to splendid temples, agora (marketplaces), and theaters. These architectural marvels served as centers of religious, social, and cultural life. The Doric and Ionic orders were prevalent in Calabrian architecture, and their influence extended to other parts of Italy as well.

The Legacy of Temples

Calabria boasts numerous ancient temples dedicated to various deities, providing a glimpse into the religious practices of the ancient Greeks. Temples such as the Temple of Hera at Lacinium and the Temple of Apollo at Kaulon bear witness to the veneration of gods and goddesses, and they continue to be sites of fascination and pilgrimage for visitors.

Philosophical Contributions

The Greek presence in Calabria also nurtured philosophical thought. Pythagoras, as mentioned earlier, played a pivotal role in the region's intellectual development. His contributions to mathematics, music, and philosophy left an enduring legacy that influenced later thinkers and contributed to the growth of knowledge in ancient and subsequent eras.

Myths and Legends

Calabria is steeped in myths and legends from ancient times. The adventures of mythical heroes, such as Hercules, Odysseus, and Jason, are intertwined with the landscapes of Calabria. The Straits of Messina, for instance, were believed to be the realm of Scylla and Charybdis, two monstrous sea creatures mentioned in Homer's "Odyssey." These myths not only added a sense of wonder to the region but also helped explain natural phenomena and events.

Conclusion

As we conclude our exploration of the ancient origins of Calabria, it becomes evident that the legacy of Magna Graecia continues to shape the region's identity and allure. From the once-thriving Greek cities of Sybaris, Croton, and Locri to the remnants of ancient temples and philosophical contributions, Calabria stands as a living testament to the richness of its past. Embracing this heritage, travelers today can immerse themselves in the captivating tales of ancient civilizations, experiencing the enduring influence of Magna Graecia in the very heart of southern Italy.

4.2 The Byzantine Influence: Monasteries and Mosaics

The Byzantine era in Calabria marked a period of cultural and artistic resurgence that left an indelible mark on the region's landscape and spirituality. In this section, we embark on a captivating journey through time, exploring the flourishing of monastic communities and the creation of awe-inspiring monasteries that stand as architectural marvels to this day. Traverse the landscapes where solitude and spirituality converged, giving rise to magnificent centers of faith that continue to inspire awe and wonder.

Monastic Flourishing in Calabria

The Byzantine era witnessed a surge in monasticism, with Calabria becoming a haven for spiritual seekers and devout believers. Monastic communities flourished, establishing their abodes amidst the lush and serene surroundings of the region. These monasteries were not only centers of religious devotion but also repositories of knowledge, preserving ancient texts and fostering artistic expression.

The Solitude of Calabrian Monasteries

Nestled amidst rugged mountains or perched on cliffs overlooking the azure sea, Calabrian monasteries were havens of solitude and contemplation. Away from the hustle and bustle of urban life, monks sought spiritual enlightenment through a life of prayer, study, and labor. As we delve into the history of these monastic communities, we uncover the profound impact they had on shaping the spiritual and cultural fabric of Calabria.

Architectural Marvels: Byzantine Monasteries

The architectural brilliance of Calabrian monasteries is a testament to the ingenuity and devotion of the Byzantine artisans who crafted them. Byzantine architecture blended elements from Roman, Greek, and Middle Eastern traditions, creating unique structures with distinct domes, intricate facades, and elaborate frescoes.

The Monastery of Santa Maria del Patire

One of the most celebrated Byzantine monasteries in Calabria is the Monastery of Santa Maria del Patire. Perched high on a rocky promontory overlooking the Ionian Sea, this majestic monastery is a masterpiece of Byzantine art and architecture. Its stunning location and panoramic views make it an ethereal place of worship and reflection.

The Monastery of San Giovanni Theristis

Hidden amidst the dense forests of Sila National Park, the Monastery of San Giovanni Theristis is a serene oasis of spirituality. Founded in the 11th century, this humble yet awe-inspiring monastery is a living testament to the devotion of the monks who sought solace and communion with the divine in this tranquil setting.

Byzantine Mosaics: Heavenly Artistry

Inside the hallowed walls of Calabrian monasteries, one encounters a breathtaking display of Byzantine mosaics. These intricate works of art depict biblical scenes, saints, angels, and heavenly realms, creating a divine ambiance that fosters a sense of transcendence and awe.

The Stories of Christ: From Birth to Resurrection

Byzantine mosaics often narrate the life of Christ, from his humble birth in a Bethlehem manger to his triumphant resurrection. The colors and designs employed in these mosaics hold symbolic significance, representing the divine majesty and spiritual truths central to Christian faith.

The Veneration of Saints

Calabrian monasteries also pay homage to revered saints and martyrs, with mosaics portraying their acts of piety and sacrifice. These representations serve as visual reminders of the holiness and virtues that the monks aspired to embody in their daily lives.

Enduring Artistry: Preserving the Past

The meticulous craftsmanship of Byzantine mosaics has allowed these artistic treasures to endure the test of time. Despite centuries of exposure to the elements and human conflicts, these intricate masterpieces continue to captivate modern viewers, providing a tangible link to the religious fervor and artistic excellence of the Byzantine era.

Conclusion

As we conclude our journey through the Byzantine era in Calabria, we are left with a profound appreciation for the cultural and spiritual legacy that this period bestowed upon the region. The flourishing of monastic communities and the creation of awe-inspiring monasteries stand as testaments to the devotion and creativity of the Byzantine era's inhabitants.

The intricate Byzantine mosaics, with their celestial depictions and vibrant colors, offer glimpses into the spiritual world that inspired generations of believers. The enduring artistry of these mosaics not only preserves the past but also serves as a source of wonder and inspiration for modern visitors.

Calabria's Byzantine heritage is a profound reflection of the region's timeless connection to spirituality, art, and cultural expression. As we contemplate the serenity and brilliance of the Byzantine era, we find ourselves drawn closer to the heart of Calabria, where history and faith intertwine, creating an eternal tapestry of wonder and contemplation.

4.3 Castles and Fortresses: Sentinels of the Past

Calabria's strategic location in the southernmost part of Italy, bordered by the Ionian and Tyrrhenian Seas, has rendered it a coveted region throughout history. This chapter takes us on a captivating journey through time, exploring the impressive castles and fortresses that stand as testament to Calabria's tumultuous past. These defensive bastions not only served to protect the region from various invaders but also represented symbols of power and authority wielded by their rulers. As we traverse the architectural evolution of these formidable structures, we uncover the stories of resilience and the battles fought within their walls.

Medieval Fortresses: Imposing Guardians

The medieval period saw the construction of numerous fortresses and castles in Calabria, with rulers vying for control of this strategic region. These fortifications were designed to withstand sieges and offer refuge to the inhabitants during times of conflict. From the high vantage points of these castles, guards kept a vigilant eye on the surrounding territories, prepared to signal an impending threat.

The Castle of Frederick II: A Royal Fortress

Among the most iconic medieval castles in Calabria is the Castle of Frederick II, situated atop a rocky hill in the town of Cosenza. Built by Emperor Frederick II in the 13th century, this fortress reflects the architectural prowess of the Swabian dynasty. Its massive walls, sturdy towers, and commanding position exemplify the defensive ingenuity of medieval military engineering.

The Fortress of Santa Severina: A Timeless Sentinel

Perched on a limestone cliff overlooking the Neto River, the Fortress of Santa Severina boasts a strategic location that made it a formidable stronghold. Originally built by the Greeks, it underwent numerous renovations by subsequent rulers, including the Normans and the Aragonese. As we explore its halls and ramparts, the echoes of battles fought and legends woven into its history resonate within its ancient stones.

Renaissance Citadels: Refinement and Strength

The Renaissance period brought about a shift in the architectural style of fortresses and castles. While still intended for defense, these structures also became showcases of refined artistic elements and luxurious living quarters for the ruling elite. Calabria's Renaissance citadels stand as testaments to this architectural transformation, reflecting the Renaissance ideals of beauty and humanism.

The Aragonese Castle of Le Castella: A Coastal Marvel

Guarding the Ionian coast, the Aragonese Castle of Le Castella boasts an imposing and elegant design that reflects the Renaissance spirit. Originally constructed by the Byzantines, the castle was later expanded and refined by the Aragonese. With its unique pentagonal shape and a moat surrounding its base, it stands as a prime example of the fusion of military defense and artistic beauty.

The Castle of Ruffo in Scilla: A Tale of Legends

The Castle of Ruffo in Scilla, perched on a rocky promontory, has earned a place in legend and lore. According to Greek mythology, the mythical sea monster Scylla once roamed the nearby waters, giving rise to the name of the town. This picturesque castle witnessed the passage of different rulers, from the Normans to the Bourbons, and its romantic setting has inspired poets and artists alike.

Battles Fought and Resilience Embodied

As we delve into the history of these castles and fortresses, we encounter tales of conquests, sieges, and the struggle for dominance. Some structures withstood numerous attacks, becoming symbols of resilience and defiance against invading forces. Other fortifications changed hands throughout history, serving as strategic assets to different rulers, each leaving their marks on the architecture and culture of Calabria.

The Siege of the Castle of Amendolea

The Castle of Amendolea, nestled amid the rugged mountains and lush greenery of southern Calabria, witnessed an epic siege in the 16th century. Spanish forces clashed with the local population in a valiant effort to hold onto their territory. The echoes of this historic battle can still be felt as visitors explore the castle's ruins and imagine the hardships faced by its defenders.

The Reconquest of Reggio Calabria

Reggio Calabria, the regional capital, was a significant prize in the struggle for control over Calabria. The Castle of Reggio Calabria, strategically located overlooking the Strait of Messina, was at the center of numerous battles. Its eventual reconquest by the Kingdom of Sicily in the 11th century marked a turning point in the region's history, as it became an important stronghold in the southern Italian defense system.

Conclusion

Calabria's castles and fortresses stand as guardians of its history and symbols of the region's resilience in the face of numerous invasions and conflicts. These awe-inspiring structures, spanning the medieval and Renaissance periods, reflect the ingenuity of military architecture and the artistic finesse of their builders.

Journeying through the architectural evolution of these formidable fortifications, we uncover the stories of battles fought, rulers who constructed them, and the enduring spirit of the people who lived within their protective walls. These castles continue to capture the imagination of modern-day travelers, transporting them back to a time of strategic maneuvering and epic tales of valor.

As we leave behind the battlements and ramparts, we carry with us the echoes of history, standing witness to the enduring power and allure of Calabria's castles and fortresses. In their majestic presence, we find a profound connection to the past, enriching our understanding of this captivating region's vibrant and storied legacy.

4.4 Archaeological Marvels: Uncovering Calabria's Past

Calabria, with its diverse landscapes and rich history, is an archaeological treasure trove that beckons explorers to delve into its ancient past. This chapter invites you on a journey of discovery, where we embark on an exciting exploration of the region's ancient sites and ruins. Archaeologists have meticulously unearthed a wealth of artifacts and historical sites that offer profound insights into the lives, beliefs, and interactions of past civilizations. From burial sites to Roman villas and once-prosperous settlements, we traverse the paths of antiquity and witness the unfolding narrative of Calabria's history.

Excavating Ancient Burial Sites

Ancient burial sites hold valuable clues about the rituals and beliefs of past civilizations. In Calabria, numerous burial grounds have been excavated, each offering a unique glimpse into the lives and afterlife beliefs of its inhabitants.

The Tomb of the Warrior Prince

One such remarkable discovery is the Tomb of the Warrior Prince in Vibo Valentia. This magnificent burial site, dating back to the 5th century BC, reveals the burial practices and reverence bestowed upon noble figures of the time. The intricately adorned grave goods and funerary offerings demonstrate the significance of warriors and nobles in Calabrian society.

Insights from Roman Villas

Calabria was once a prominent region in the Roman Empire, boasting luxurious villas that served as elegant residences for the elite. Excavations of these grand villas have provided invaluable insights into Roman lifestyles, architecture, and artistic expressions.

The Roman Villa of Casignana

The Roman Villa of Casignana, nestled amidst the countryside, offers a vivid picture of Roman opulence and culture. Intricate mosaics, vibrant frescoes, and well-preserved architectural elements showcase the refined taste and artistry of its former inhabitants. As we walk through the corridors of time, we gain an appreciation for the sophistication and elegance that defined Roman living.

Remnants of Once-Prosperous Settlements

The ancient settlements of Calabria were vibrant hubs of trade, culture, and innovation. The remains of these once-thriving communities provide valuable insights into the urban planning, social structures, and artistic achievements of their respective eras.

The Archaeological Park of Scolacium

The Archaeological Park of Scolacium, near the present-day town of Squillace, is an exceptional example of a prosperous ancient settlement. Once a bustling Roman city known as Scylletium, it later thrived under Byzantine rule. The well-preserved amphitheater, forum, and basilica are testaments to its former glory, offering a window into the lives of its inhabitants throughout the ages.

Rewriting the Narrative: Unveiling New Mysteries

Archaeology is an ever-evolving field, and modern research methods continue to uncover new mysteries and revise our understanding of the past. Calabria's archaeological sites are not only snapshots of history but also ongoing sources of inquiry and discovery.

The Mystery of the Riace Bronzes

Among the most iconic archaeological discoveries in Calabria are the Riace Bronzes, two remarkable ancient Greek sculptures representing warriors. Unearthed in 1972, these larger-than-life bronzes have puzzled scholars with their exquisite craftsmanship and uncertain origins. Their discovery has sparked debates and new theories, reshaping our perception of ancient art and its diffusion.

The Calabrian Greek Legacy

Calabria's Greek heritage is evident in its dialects, traditions, and archaeological findings. Ancient Greek colonies left an indelible mark on the region, and the exploration of their legacy continues to shed light on the intercultural exchanges that shaped Calabria's identity.

The Preservation of Calabria's Heritage

Preserving and safeguarding Calabria's archaeological sites is an ongoing endeavor. Excavations, restoration projects, and public awareness initiatives play crucial roles in ensuring that these cultural treasures endure for future generations.

Conclusion

As we conclude our journey through Calabria's archaeological marvels, we gain a deeper appreciation for the region's historical significance and the lasting impact of past civilizations on its art, culture, and architecture. The exploration of ancient burial sites, Roman villas, and once-thriving settlements paints a vivid picture of the diverse tapestry of history woven into Calabria's landscapes.

Archaeology is a discipline of continuous discovery and reinterpretation, and Calabria's past continues to be rewritten as new mysteries are unveiled. From the enigmatic Riace Bronzes to the enduring legacy of Calabrian Greek heritage, the region's archaeological wonders captivate the imagination and beckon travelers to delve into its captivating history.

In this captivating corner of Italy, the exploration of ancient origins, Byzantine influence, castles, and archaeological marvels enriches the travel experience, immersing visitors in the timeless allure of Calabria's past. As we walk in the footsteps of past civilizations, we connect with the enduring spirit of the region, embracing its heritage as a precious testament to human history and cultural evolution.

CHAPTER FIVE

Calabria's Rich Cultural Heritage

5.1 Folk Music and Dance: A Celebration of Life

In the heart of Calabria, the vibrant rhythm of folk music and dance resounds through the towns and villages, embodying the spirit of the region's people. In this chapter, we delve into the rich musical heritage that has been passed down through generations, representing a celebration of life and the unique cultural identity of Calabria.

The Origins of Folk Music: Calabrian folk music stands as a testament to the region's deep and diverse cultural history, with its origins reaching far back into antiquity. To truly understand the essence of this musical art form, we journey through time, unraveling the historical roots that have shaped its evolution and contributed to its soul-stirring melodies.

Ancient Beginnings: The roots of Calabrian folk music can be traced to the ancient civilizations that once flourished in the region, including the Greeks, Romans, Byzantines, and even the indigenous Italic tribes. These cultures brought with them their unique musical traditions, instruments, and poetic expressions, laying the foundation for what would later become the distinctive Calabrian musical heritage.

Crossroads of Civilization: Over the centuries, Calabria served as a crossroads for various civilizations and cultures, making it a melting pot of musical influences. The interactions between diverse communities led to a fascinating fusion of styles, resulting in a rich tapestry of melodies that became the essence of Calabrian folk music.

The Impact of Migration: The history of Calabria is marked by waves of emigration, where countless Calabrians sought new opportunities in distant lands. As they carried their traditions with them, their music became a bridge that connected them to their homeland. This diaspora not only preserved Calabrian folk music but also spread its influence to far-flung corners of the world.

Instruments of the Soul: A vital aspect of Calabrian folk music lies in its use of traditional instruments that have been passed down through generations. From the rustic and soulful sound of the bagpipes, like the zampogna and ciaramedda, to the tambourines and mandolins that accompany lively dances, each instrument holds a unique place in the collective heart of the Calabrian people.

The Evolution of Themes and Lyrics: Calabrian folk music reflects the daily lives, struggles, and joys of the region's inhabitants. Songs often revolve around themes of love, work, nature, and local legends, capturing the essence of everyday existence. The poetic and emotional lyrics provide insight into the hopes, dreams, and aspirations of generations past, creating an enduring connection with the present.

Preserving a Living Tradition: Despite the passage of time, Calabrian folk music has managed to endure through the efforts of passionate musicians, scholars, and cultural enthusiasts. Local festivals, events, and gatherings continue to showcase the beauty of these age-old melodies, ensuring that the soulful tunes of Calabria resonate with new generations.

In immersing ourselves in the historical roots of Calabrian folk music, we gain a profound appreciation for the enduring legacy that has been passed down through the ages. The captivating blend of ancient influences and cross-cultural exchanges has birthed a musical tradition that remains deeply rooted in the hearts of the Calabrian people, keeping their cultural heritage alive for generations to come.

Local Musical Traditions:

As we traverse the picturesque landscapes and charming towns of Calabria, we embark on a musical journey like no other, encountering a plethora of musical styles that mirror the region's vibrant cultural tapestry. Each melodic treasure we discover holds a captivating story, reflecting the diverse facets of Calabria's history, traditions, and the very essence of its people.

The Joyful Tarantella: Among the most iconic and lively musical expressions of Calabria is the exuberant tarantella. As we join in the festivities during special occasions and traditional celebrations, the infectious rhythms of this dance lead us in joyful revelry. The tarantella's origins can be traced back to ancient rituals associated with the mythical bite of the tarantula spider, believed to be cured through frenetic dancing. Today, this vivacious dance represents the spirit of togetherness and is a testament to the resilience and passion of the Calabrian people.

The Haunting Zampogna: Amidst the serene landscapes of Calabria's pastoral countryside, the soulful notes of the zampogna resonate, taking us back to the ancient traditions of the region's shepherds. This iconic shepherd's bagpipe carries with it a haunting beauty, evoking the quietude of the countryside and the deep connection between man and nature. As we listen to the melodic lament of the zampogna, we sense the echoes of time-honored pastoral lifestyles and the enduring bond between Calabrians and their rural heritage.

The Ballads of Love and Longing: Alongside the energetic dances, we discover tender ballads that convey the profound emotions of love, heartbreak, and longing. These heartfelt songs, often accompanied by acoustic instruments like the mandolin, recount tales of love stories, unrequited passions, and the bittersweet experiences of life. Their poetic verses offer a window into the intimate and sentimental aspects of Calabrian culture, showcasing the poetic prowess of the region's troubadours.

The Rhythmic Tambourines: No celebration in Calabria is complete without the rhythmic beats of tambourines, adding a lively pulse to the festivities. The dynamic interplay between the tambourines and the melodies of other traditional instruments infuses the air with energy and excitement. Whether it's during a religious procession, a village festa, or a spontaneous gathering, the rhythmic sounds of tambourines unite the community in a shared spirit of celebration.

A Harmonious Fusion: As we delve deeper into the musical landscape of Calabria, we encounter instances where the region's melodies merge with influences from neighboring cultures and beyond. From traces of Greek melodies reminiscent of Magna Graecia to echoes of North African rhythms, these intercultural exchanges enrich the musical heritage of Calabria, making it a living testament to the region's historical crossroads.

In uncovering this diverse array of musical expressions, we not only immerse ourselves in the captivating sounds of Calabria but also gain insight into the multifaceted identities and cultural bonds that have shaped this enchanting region. The melodies of Calabria, with their compelling stories and emotional depth, provide an enduring testament to the timeless allure of this corner of Italy and the enduring spirit of its people.

Dancing to the Rhythm: In Calabria, the art of dance is woven into the very fabric of life, serving as a vibrant expression of the region's rich cultural heritage. As we wander through its enchanting streets and bustling piazzas, we are swept up in the rhythmic beats and graceful movements of the exuberant folk dances that enliven every celebration. These captivating spectacles unite the community, drawing us closer to the essence of Calabria's collective spirit.

Embracing the "N'drezzata" Sword Dance: Stepping into a local gathering, we are mesmerized by the sight of the "N'drezzata," a traditional sword dance that holds deep symbolic significance. Dancers, adorned in colorful traditional attire, expertly wield swords as they weave intricate patterns in unison. This ritualistic performance, passed down through generations, showcases the valor and unity of the Calabrian people. The "N'drezzata" is not merely a dance but a portrayal of history, recounting tales of ancient battles and the unyielding strength of community bonds.

Captivated by the "Pizzica" Healing Dance: As the sun sets and the moon casts a soft glow upon the festivities, we are drawn to the mesmerizing rhythms of the "Pizzica." Originating from the belief that a tarantula's bite could induce a trance-like state, this captivating dance is said to heal those affected by the venom. The dancers, moving with passion and abandon, twirl and sway to the haunting melody of the tambourines and mandolins. It is as if they are in communion with a hidden force, transcending the boundaries of time and space. The "Pizzica" dance embodies the resilience of the Calabrian spirit and its ability to transform adversity into jubilation.

A Tapestry of Unity and Joy: Through these dances, we witness the threads of unity and joy that bind the Calabrian people together. Young and old, locals and visitors, all become participants in the age-old tradition of dance. As the infectious rhythms and melodies permeate the air, barriers dissolve, and a sense of shared camaraderie envelops everyone present. The collective joy of the dancers mirrors the joy of the community, encapsulating the essence of Calabria's warm and welcoming spirit.

Preserving Cultural Heritage: As we watch the dance groups perform with unwavering dedication and skill, we recognize the importance of preserving these time-honored traditions. Local dance schools and community organizations play a crucial role in passing down the art of dance to future generations, ensuring that the dances of Calabria continue to enchant and inspire.

In the vibrant art of dance, we find a window into the soul of Calabria, a region defined by its sense of togetherness, resilience, and passion for life. With the "N'drezzata" and the "Pizzica" as our guides, we partake in the unifying joy that these dances bring, leaving us with lasting memories of the dynamic spirit that permeates every corner of this charming southern Italian gem.

5.2 The Art of Handicrafts: Local Artisans at Work

In the villages and towns of Calabria, a centuries-old tradition of craftsmanship lives on, as skilled artisans pour their heart and soul into creating exquisite handmade works of art. This section immerses us in the world of Calabrian handicrafts, exploring the dedication and creativity of local artisans.

The Legacy of Craftsmanship: As we delve into the world of Calabrian handicrafts, we find ourselves transported through the annals of time, tracing the origins of these traditional arts back to ancient civilizations. The enduring legacy of these crafts is a testament to the region's ingenuity, creativity, and unwavering commitment to preserving its cultural heritage.

Craftsmanship Through the Ages: The history of Calabrian handicrafts dates back thousands of years, with roots intertwined with the rise of ancient civilizations that settled in the area. From the Greeks and Romans to the Byzantines and Normans, each influential culture left its indelible mark on the artisanal traditions of the region. Calabria's strategic position at the crossroads of different civilizations facilitated the exchange of techniques, materials, and designs, resulting in a diverse array of crafts unique to the region.

Preserving Cultural Identity: Handicrafts in Calabria have always been more than just functional objects; they carry deep cultural significance, embodying the essence of the region's identity. From the terracotta pottery of the Magna Graecia era to the intricate weaving patterns inspired by Byzantine motifs, each craft reflects the multifaceted history and artistic ingenuity of the Calabrian people. Passed down through generations, these artisanal skills are a source of pride, connecting modern artisans with their ancestors and maintaining a vital link to the past.

Pottery: In the art of pottery, we find echoes of ancient rituals, utilitarian vessels, and ornate decorations that tell stories of daily life and religious practices. The skilled hands of potters shape clay into exquisite amphorae, vases, and ceramics, carrying on age-old techniques that have stood the test of time.

Woodworking: From the intricate carvings adorning religious statues to the sturdy wooden furniture embellishing homes, woodworking in Calabria reveals the region's craftsmanship at its finest. The use of local wood, such as olive, chestnut, and pine, imparts a distinct character to each piece, while the mastery of carving techniques demonstrates the skill and dedication of the artisans.

Textile Weaving: Textile weaving, another ancient craft, exemplifies the fusion of cultures that have influenced

Calabria over the centuries. Looms come alive as weavers create splendid fabrics and traditional garments adorned with vibrant patterns and colors. The textiles not only serve as clothing but also carry stories of familial ties, customs, and celebrations.

Leatherworking: The art of leatherworking showcases Calabria's resourcefulness in utilizing natural materials to craft durable and beautiful items. Leather artisans skillfully fashion belts, shoes, bags, and intricately tooled objects that pay homage to the region's rural and equestrian traditions.

Sustaining Tradition: Despite the challenges posed by modernity, Calabrian artisans, deeply aware of the historical significance of their crafts, have embraced the role of cultural ambassadors. Through apprenticeships and workshops, they ensure that their skills are passed on to the next generation, preserving the legacy of these crafts for years to come.

In exploring the historical significance of Calabrian handicrafts, we gain a profound appreciation for the artistic ingenuity and cultural pride that have shaped these timeless traditions. These artisanal treasures serve as a living testament to the vibrant heritage of Calabria, where the spirit of creativity and craftsmanship continues to thrive in harmony with its storied past.

Meet the Artisans: As we step into the enchanting world of Calabrian craftsmanship, we are privileged to meet some of the region's most talented and dedicated artisans. These skilled individuals have devoted their lives to honing their craft, and their workshops become havens of creativity and tradition, where the magic of artistic expression comes to life.

A Meeting of Masters: Our journey introduces us to artisans who have inherited their craft from preceding generations, their skills passed down through time-honored family traditions. We are welcomed into their workshops with warm smiles and open hearts, eager to share their stories and passion for their chosen art forms.

The Potter's Tale: In the pottery atelier, we encounter the potter, whose hands mold raw clay into captivating forms. The artisan shares insights into the history of Calabrian pottery, explaining how the ancient techniques have been preserved and adapted through the ages. We witness the potter's mastery as they deftly shape vases, amphorae, and ornate ceramics, each piece bearing a unique artistic touch.

A Woodcarver's Artistry: In another corner of Calabria's artisan community, we find the woodcarver's workshop, where the scent of freshly carved wood fills the air. Here, the woodcarver reveals the secrets of intricate carving techniques, showcasing the diversity of designs inspired by Calabrian folklore, religious motifs, and the region's natural beauty. We observe in awe as delicate details emerge from blocks of wood, bringing forth awe-inspiring sculptures and finely crafted furniture.

The Weaver's World: The weaver invites us into their textile studio, a treasure trove of colorful threads and intricate looms. This artisan's hands skillfully interlace the threads, creating fabrics that tell stories through ancient patterns and designs. We are immersed in the narrative of the region's cultural heritage as the weaver shares the symbolism and significance behind each woven masterpiece.

The Leather Artisan's Touch: In the leatherworker's sanctuary, the air is filled with the aroma of tanned leather. Here, the artisan demonstrates the meticulous process of transforming raw hides into finely crafted belts, shoes, and accessories. The leatherworker's precision and attention to detail highlight the deep respect for the material and its connection to Calabria's rural heritage.

A Passionate Journey: In the presence of these passionate artisans, we witness not only the technical mastery of their crafts but also the emotional connection they have with their art. Their dedication shines through every piece they create, reflecting their love for their craft and a commitment to preserving Calabria's cultural legacy.

Keeping the Flame Alive: As we bid farewell to these skilled artisans, we are left with a profound appreciation for their tireless efforts to carry on the traditions of their ancestors. Their commitment to passing down their expertise to the next generation ensures that the flame of creativity and craftsmanship will continue to burn brightly in Calabria for generations to come.

In the workshops of these talented artisans, we have encountered not just masterpieces but also the very essence of Calabria's artistic soul. Their work is a living testament to the region's rich cultural heritage and a testament to the enduring spirit of creativity that flourishes within the heart of this enchanting corner of Italy.

Traditional Techniques: As we delve into the fascinating world of Calabrian craftsmanship, we find ourselves on a captivating journey into the intricacies of traditional techniques, which have been carefully handed down through the ages, from one skilled generation to the next. Each art form is a testament to the dedication and expertise of these artisans, preserving the essence of Calabria's cultural heritage.

The Delicate Art of Lace-Making: In the quiet corners of Calabria, we discover the timeless art of lace-making, a craft that demands both patience and precision. The lace-makers deftly weave delicate threads into intricate patterns, creating stunning masterpieces that exude elegance and grace. Passed down from mothers to daughters, the secrets of lace-making embody the stories of generations past, as each new lace-maker adds their unique touch to the ancient art form.

The Artistry of Pottery Glazing: In the pottery workshops, we witness the alchemy of glazing, where skilled hands carefully apply vibrant colors and intricate designs to the clay masterpieces. The glazing process involves a delicate balance of technique and intuition, as artisans select the perfect hues to enhance the form and bring life to their creations. Through this time-honored practice, they pay homage to the rich history of Calabrian pottery and the profound connection it holds to the land and its people.

The Time-Honored Methods of Producing Intricate Textiles: In the bustling textile ateliers, we are immersed in the world of weaving and spinning, where artisans employ centuries-old techniques to produce exquisite fabrics. The rhythmic clatter of looms and the careful interlacing of threads create beautiful textiles adorned with patterns inspired by nature, folklore, and religious symbolism. Here, we witness the blending of old and new, as modern designs are woven using traditional methods, keeping the legacy of textile craftsmanship alive in Calabria.

The Bond Between Artisan and Material: Each art form reveals a profound connection between the artisan and their chosen material. As we watch the lace-makers gently caress fine threads, the potters shape the supple clay, and the weavers guide the threads through their looms, we witness a dance of mastery and reverence. The materials themselves seem to respond to the artisan's touch, yielding to the guiding hand and taking on new life in the hands of these skilled creators.

The Storytelling in Craftsmanship: Beyond the technical expertise, we recognize that each crafted piece carries a story, a narrative of Calabria's history, culture, and collective memory. The motifs in lace, the glazes on pottery, and the patterns in textiles tell tales of ancient traditions, spiritual beliefs, and the relationship between the people and the land. The artisans' works become vessels of storytelling, connecting the present with the past and bridging the generations.

Passing the Torch: Throughout our journey, we witness the artisans' commitment to passing on their craft to the next generation. In apprenticeships and workshops, they patiently share their knowledge and skills, ensuring that these precious traditions endure. The continuity of craftsmanship not only preserves the techniques but also kindles the creative spark in young hearts, ensuring that Calabria's cultural heritage remains vibrant for the years ahead.

In exploring the intricacies of these traditional techniques, we uncover a profound appreciation for the dedication and artistry of Calabrian artisans. Their skills, rooted in the past yet open to the future, weave an extraordinary tapestry of cultural identity and artistic brilliance that enriches the very soul of Calabria.

Supporting Local Artisans: In recent years, there has been a growing awareness of the importance of preserving traditional crafts and the cultural heritage they represent. Efforts to safeguard these artistic traditions have not only fostered sustainable tourism in Calabria but also created valuable economic opportunities for local communities. Through various initiatives, visitors are encouraged to invest in authentic handcrafted products, ensuring the continuation of these ancient arts and providing a lifeline for the artisans and their communities.

Craftsmanship as a Cultural Asset: Calabria's rich cultural heritage, deeply entwined with its traditional crafts, has been recognized as a unique cultural asset. Local governments and cultural organizations have taken proactive steps to promote and protect these crafts, appreciating their significance in preserving the region's identity. By showcasing the artistry and history behind each craft, they kindle interest and curiosity among tourists, attracting travelers who seek authentic and meaningful experiences.

Craft Tours and Workshops: Sustainable tourism initiatives have curated craft tours and workshops that immerse visitors in the world of Calabrian artisans. These experiences allow travelers to witness the craftsmanship firsthand, from raw materials to the finished products. Engaging with the artisans not only educates visitors about the intricate processes but also builds a deeper connection between the creators and their audience.

Supporting Artisan Markets: Artisan markets and craft fairs have become vibrant hubs for the exchange of culture and ideas. Local artisans come together to showcase their creations, allowing visitors to purchase unique handmade products directly from the artists themselves. These markets create a direct link between the artisans and consumers, fostering a sense of appreciation and understanding of the craftsmanship involved.

Promoting Ethical and Sustainable Consumption: Sustainable tourism initiatives emphasize the importance of ethical and sustainable consumption. Travelers are encouraged to invest in high-quality, locally crafted products rather than mass-produced souvenirs. By doing so, they not only take home authentic pieces of Calabria's culture but also contribute to the well-being of the artisans and their communities.

Social Enterprises and Cooperatives: Social enterprises and cooperatives have emerged as powerful agents of change, supporting artisans and fostering economic empowerment. These initiatives offer fair wages, safe working conditions, and opportunities for skill development to artisans, ensuring that their crafts remain viable sources of income. Visitors are encouraged to support these enterprises, knowing that their purchases have a positive social impact.

Cultural Exchange Programs: Cultural exchange programs facilitate interactions between local artisans and international artists. Through these exchanges, diverse creative influences merge, inspiring innovation while preserving traditional techniques. Such programs also create a platform for artists to showcase their crafts on a global stage, expanding the reach and appreciation of Calabrian craftsmanship beyond its borders.

Building Cultural Bridges: Sustainable tourism has become a powerful tool in bridging cultural gaps and fostering mutual understanding. Visitors from different parts of the world appreciate the beauty and significance of Calabrian crafts, and artisans, in turn, gain exposure to diverse perspectives and artistic influences. This cultural exchange enriches both the artisans and the travelers, creating a dynamic and interconnected world of creativity.

In these ways, the preservation of traditional crafts in Calabria has become a driving force behind sustainable tourism and community development. The support and appreciation of visitors not only sustain the livelihoods of artisans but also ensure that these ancient arts continue to thrive, carrying forward the spirit of Calabria's cultural heritage for generations to come.

5.3 Religious Festivals: Embracing Tradition and Faith

Religion holds a profound place in the hearts of the Calabrian people, and the region is home to a multitude of religious festivals that blend ancient traditions with Christian beliefs. In this section, we participate in the lively and deeply spiritual religious celebrations that define the cultural tapestry of Calabria.

The Intersection of Faith and Culture: As we delve into the world of Calabria's vibrant festivals, we find ourselves immersed in a tapestry of history and faith, where ancient pagan rites intermingle with Christian traditions, creating a unique and captivating cultural landscape. These festivals embody the harmonious blend of sacred and secular elements, where the past and the present coalesce to form the foundation of these extraordinary events.

Ancient Roots and Pagan Traditions: Many of Calabria's festivals can be traced back to ancient pagan celebrations, rooted in the rhythms of nature and the cycles of life. These ancient rites, often tied to agricultural seasons and celestial events, were an intrinsic part of the lives of the region's inhabitants. With the advent of Christianity, these pagan festivities became intertwined with Christian feasts, providing a seamless connection between the region's pre-Christian past and its Christian present.

The Influence of Christianity: Christian feasts and religious traditions took root in Calabria over the centuries, adding new layers of meaning to the existing festivals. Each event became an opportunity to commemorate saints, martyrs, and significant moments in the life of Jesus Christ. The inclusion of Christian elements into these celebrations not only enriched the festivities but also provided a framework for the region's religious identity.

The Sacred and the Profane in Celebration: Calabria's festivals are marked by a fascinating juxtaposition of the sacred and the profane. Religious processions, solemn ceremonies, and devotional rituals are interspersed with lively music, colorful costumes, and exuberant dances. This seamless intermingling of sacred and secular elements reflects the deep-rooted belief that spirituality is not confined to places of worship but rather permeates every aspect of life.

Commemorating History and Tradition: Each festival carries historical and cultural significance, commemorating events that shaped the region's identity. From the triumph of good over evil to the remembrance of historical figures and battles, the festivals serve as living repositories of the region's past. They become moments of collective memory, uniting the community in shared stories and traditions that have been passed down through generations.

Bringing the Community Together: These captivating festivals are not just religious events but also communal gatherings that foster a strong sense of unity. Families, friends, and neighbors come together, creating a sense of belonging and camaraderie. The festivities transcend age, social status, and backgrounds, weaving a sense of community that strengthens the bonds among the people of Calabria.

Perpetuating Cultural Heritage: The continuation of these festivals is a testament to the resilience of Calabria's cultural heritage. Each passing year, the torch is carried forward, with new generations actively participating in the festivities. The commitment to preserving these traditions ensures that the legacy of the region's ancestors lives on, making Calabria's cultural heritage an ever-evolving and timeless tapestry.

As we witness the harmonious blend of historical and religious elements in these captivating events, we come to appreciate the profound cultural significance they hold for the people of Calabria. These festivals stand as living testimonies to the region's past, reflecting the enduring spirit of its inhabitants, and showcasing the beautiful symphony of traditions that continues to flourish in the present day.

Easter Celebrations: In Calabria, Holy Week is a time of deep spiritual significance and profound emotion, as the faithful gather to commemorate the Passion of Christ. Throughout this sacred period, processions and rituals unfold, creating an atmosphere of solemnity and reflection that resonates with the hearts of the Calabrian people.

A Journey through Good Friday Processions: Among the most awe-inspiring events of Holy Week is the extraordinary Good Friday procession. As the sun sets, the streets of Calabrian towns and villages become illuminated by the gentle glow of countless candles and the vibrant colors of fragrant flowers. The air is filled with a palpable sense of reverence and devotion as the faithful gather to participate in this solemn ritual.

Biblical Scenes Come to Life: The heart of the Good Friday procession lies in the ornate and elaborately crafted statues that depict pivotal moments from the Passion of Christ. These lifelike figures, sculpted with remarkable detail, portray scenes such as the Last Supper, the Betrayal of

Judas, the Carrying of the Cross, and the Crucifixion. Each statue becomes a tangible embodiment of the biblical narrative, allowing the faithful to witness the events of Christ's final moments with their own eyes.

A Sea of Candles and Flowers: As the statues are carried through the streets, they are accompanied by a sea of flickering candles, casting a soft glow that seems to envelop the procession in an ethereal aura. The cobbled pathways are adorned with a colorful tapestry of flower petals, symbolizing both mourning and hope, as the faithful pay homage to Christ's sacrifice.

The Sounds of Devotion: The air is filled with solemn hymns and prayers sung by the participants, creating an atmosphere of profound reverence and piety. The collective voices of the faithful, united in song and prayer, echo through the streets, carrying their heartfelt emotions and devotion to the heavens above.

Expressions of Faith and Community: The Good Friday procession is not only a deeply spiritual event but also a powerful symbol of community and shared faith. Families, neighbors, and friends come together to take part in this ancient tradition, forming a unified and supportive community of believers. As the statues pass through the streets, the faithful express their devotion by showering them with rose petals and offering silent prayers, creating a powerful sense of collective worship and unity.

A Time for Reflection and Renewal: For the people of Calabria, the Good Friday procession offers a time for introspection and renewal of faith. It is a moment to remember Christ's sacrifice, to contemplate the universal themes of redemption and forgiveness, and to draw strength and inspiration from the example of His unyielding love.

In the profound emotions of Calabria's Holy Week, we find a profound spiritual journey that speaks to the depths of the human soul. The Good Friday procession, with its artistry, devotion, and sense of community, serves as a poignant reminder of the enduring power of faith and the timeless traditions that continue to shape the cultural fabric of Calabria.

Patron Saint Festivals: In Calabria, the spirit of devotion and celebration is deeply ingrained in the fabric of daily life, as each town and village holds its patron saint in high esteem. Throughout the year, the feast days of these revered figures are eagerly anticipated and celebrated with great fervor, uniting the community in a joyous display of faith and heritage. Joining in the festivities, we immerse ourselves in the rich tapestry of religious processions, traditional music, and communal feasts that honor these beloved patron saints.

Anticipation and Preparation: As the feast day of the patron saint approaches, a sense of excitement permeates the air in Calabrian towns and villages. The faithful prepare for the celebrations with meticulous attention to detail, adorning the streets with colorful banners, elaborate decorations, and fragrant flowers. Each community takes pride in creating an atmosphere of warmth and devotion that mirrors their unwavering reverence for their patron saint.

Religious Processions: The heart of the festivities lies in the religious processions, where the statue of the patron saint takes center stage. Bedecked in resplendent robes and adorned with precious jewels, the statue is carefully placed on an ornate carriage. As the procession commences, the faithful gather, their hearts brimming with reverence and gratitude. The streets come alive with the rhythmic sound of drums and trumpets, as the devotees walk in solemnity and devotion, carrying candles and incense as symbols of their faith.

Traditional Music and Dance: The air resonates with the soulful melodies of traditional music, as local bands and musicians accompany the processions. Folkloric dances, each with its own unique steps and symbolism, fill the streets with an enchanting display of cultural heritage. The harmonious blend of sacred hymns and lively dances reflects the balance between the spiritual and the secular in Calabria's festive celebrations.

Community Feasts and Gatherings: Following the religious processions, the celebration continues with communal feasts, known as "pranzi" or "cenoni," where families and friends come together to share a bountiful meal. Tables are laden with an array of delectable dishes, reflecting the region's culinary diversity and cultural pride. These communal gatherings foster a sense of unity and camaraderie, as people of all ages bond over their shared devotion and love for their patron saint.

Devotion in Generations: The feast days of patron saints in Calabria hold a timeless appeal, transcending generations and forging a powerful connection between past and present. Elderly members of the community, with their deep-rooted memories, pass down stories of ancient traditions to the young, ensuring that the spirit of devotion remains alive in the hearts of future generations.

A Celebration of Faith and Heritage: As we partake in the festivities, we witness a celebration that goes beyond mere rituals; it is a testament to the resilience of faith and the enduring power of cultural heritage. The devotion to patron saints in Calabria is a living expression of the region's identity, an affirmation of the deep-rooted bond between the people and their spiritual protectors.

In the joyous celebrations of feast days, we discover the profound connection between faith, community, and tradition in Calabria. The devotion and love for patron saints are a testament to the enduring spirit of this enchanting region, where the past and the present converge in a vibrant celebration of faith, unity, and cultural legacy.

Rituals and Symbolism:

In the religious festivals of Calabria, we encounter a rich tapestry of symbolic elements that trace their origins to ancient traditions and beliefs. Each ritual and symbol carries profound meanings, bridging the gap between the past and the present, and connecting the people of Calabria with their spiritual roots.

Symbols of Fertility and Rebirth: Many of the festivals in Calabria are rooted in ancient agricultural rites, symbolizing the cycles of nature and the renewal of life. The use of colorful flowers, such as lilies and roses, signifies the arrival of spring and the promise of new beginnings. These symbols of fertility and rebirth are woven into the religious processions, evoking a sense of hope and rejuvenation as the community celebrates its spiritual heritage.

The Triumph of Good over Evil: At the heart of many religious festivals lies the theme of the triumph of good over evil. This symbolic battle is often depicted through dramatic reenactments of biblical events, such as the Crucifixion and the Resurrection of Christ. These performances become powerful allegories of the eternal struggle between darkness and light, providing a poignant reminder of the enduring power of faith and goodness.

The Significance of Fire: Fire holds deep symbolic significance in Calabria's religious festivals, representing purification, transformation, and the divine presence. Candles, torches, and bonfires are integral parts of the processions, illuminating the way as the statues of patron saints are carried through the streets. The flickering flames symbolize the eternal light of faith, dispelling darkness and bringing forth spiritual enlightenment.

Floral Offerings: Flowers have been revered as symbols of devotion and purity since ancient times. In Calabria's religious festivals, the offering of flowers to the patron saints is an act of reverence and gratitude. The delicate petals and vibrant colors are seen as expressions of love and adoration, representing the devotion of the faithful towards their spiritual protectors.

Religious Icons and Statues: The statues of patron saints and religious icons play a central role in the festivals. These sculpted representations hold deep spiritual meaning, serving as tangible connections between the earthly realm and the divine. Carried in processions, these statues become vessels of sacred energy, drawing the faithful into a transcendent experience that links them to the spiritual realm.

Water and Purification: Water is another elemental symbol that features prominently in Calabrian religious rituals. From the purification of participants during processions to the blessings bestowed upon the congregation, water holds a cleansing and sanctifying role in the festivities. The act of sprinkling or immersing oneself in holy water represents a symbolic cleansing of the soul and a reaffirmation of one's faith.

The Power of Communal Gatherings: The very act of coming together as a community to celebrate these festivals is symbolic in itself. The shared rituals, prayers, and feasts foster a sense of unity and oneness, reaffirming the collective identity of the people of Calabria. Through these communal gatherings, the spiritual roots of the region are nourished and sustained, passing on the traditions and symbols from one generation to the next.

In delving into the symbolic elements of Calabria's religious festivals, we are granted a glimpse into the profound meanings and deep-rooted connections that underlie these cherished celebrations. Each ritual and symbol serves as a thread that weaves together the tapestry of faith, heritage, and cultural identity, enriching the spiritual experience and strengthening the bond among the people of Calabria.

By embracing the cultural expressions of folk music and dance, exploring the time-honored craftsmanship, and participating in the religious festivals, travelers can gain a deeper appreciation for the soul of Calabria and its people.

CHAPTER SIX

Indulging in Calabrian Cuisine

6.1 A Gastronomic Journey: Tasting Calabria's Flavors

Embark on a delightful gastronomic journey through the heart of Calabria, a land where culinary traditions have been woven into the fabric of daily life for centuries. Calabrian cuisine is an exquisite tapestry of flavors, shaped by the region's history, geography, and the passion of its people. As you traverse this culinary wonderland, each dish becomes a portal to the past, narrating tales of ancient civilizations, trade routes, and cultural influences that have left their mark on the region's culinary identity.

At the core of Calabrian gastronomy lies a harmonious blend of Mediterranean flavors, a reflection of the abundance provided by the land and the bounty of the surrounding sea. The local cuisine celebrates simplicity and authenticity, with a focus on fresh, locally sourced produce and time-honored cooking techniques passed down through generations.

One of the defining characteristics of Calabrian cuisine is the sheer diversity of ingredients and dishes found across the region's varied landscape. From the sun-kissed plains that yield an abundance of fruits, vegetables, and grains to the rugged mountains with their sheep and goats that supply milk and cheese, and the pristine coastline teeming with a rich variety of seafood, each area contributes its own culinary treasures.

In the picturesque coastal town of Tropea, you'll encounter a bounty of red onions, sweet and vibrant, lending their distinctive flavor to local dishes. The region's fertile soil also gives rise to succulent tomatoes, peppers, eggplants, and zucchini that form the foundation of many traditional recipes. Wander further inland, and you'll discover the rugged mountains of Sila, where hearty lamb and goat dishes take center stage, infused with fragrant herbs for an irresistible aroma.

Calabrian cuisine's close ties to the sea are evident in dishes like the iconic Pasta with Swordfish, a true testament to the region's fusion of land and sea. Here, fresh swordfish is complemented with tomatoes, capers, olives, and a hint of chili pepper, capturing the essence of the Ionian coast on a plate. The Calabrian tradition of preserving fish dates back centuries, and this dish is a reflection of the resourcefulness of the local fishermen and the profound respect for the sea.

As you journey deeper into the heart of Calabria, the mountainous region of Aspromonte reveals its culinary gems, including the world-renowned 'Nduja. This soft and spicy spreadable salami is made from locally sourced pork, seasoned with fiery Calabrian chili peppers, and left to age to perfection. 'Nduja not only showcases the region's mastery of charcuterie but also embodies the Calabrian spirit - bold, vibrant, and full of character.

A gastronomic journey through Calabria goes beyond the palate; it's an exploration of the region's history and cultural influences that have left an indelible mark on its culinary heritage. Traces of ancient civilizations, including the Greeks and Romans, can be found in the intricate spice blends, the use of aromatic herbs, and the appreciation for simple, unadulterated flavors.

In addition to the historical influences, Calabrian cuisine also bears witness to the region's strategic location along ancient trade routes. Throughout history, Calabria has been a melting pot of diverse cultures, and this cultural exchange is reflected in its dishes. Arab traders introduced almonds and citrus fruits to the region, which are now integral to many Calabrian desserts and pastries. The Spanish brought new spices and techniques, enriching the local culinary repertoire.

The significance of fresh, locally sourced produce in Calabrian cooking cannot be overstated. The region's rich agricultural heritage is cherished, and many families still maintain their own gardens, cultivating traditional vegetables and herbs with love and care. The close connection to the land is evident in the daily rituals of gathering ingredients for meals, transforming cooking into a deeply rooted cultural practice.

Traditional methods, passed down through generations, remain a cornerstone of Calabrian cuisine. Time-honored practices, such as sun-drying tomatoes or curing olives, not only preserve the abundance of the harvest but also enhance the flavors, resulting in uniquely intense tastes that define Calabrian dishes.

The essence of Calabrian cuisine lies in the delicate balance of flavors, where simplicity reigns supreme. Many traditional recipes boast only a handful of ingredients, yet each one is chosen with precision to create a symphony of taste. The art of balancing sweet and savory, spicy and mellow, is a skill that has been honed by Calabrian cooks over centuries.

The spirit of Calabria is interwoven into every dish, from the soul-warming stews that offer comfort during winter to the refreshing salads that provide relief from the summer sun. A meal in Calabria is more than sustenance; it is an experience that connects you to the land, the sea, and the people who have lovingly prepared it.

In conclusion, embarking on a gastronomic journey through Calabria offers more than just a feast for the senses; it is an immersion into the heart and soul of a region deeply rooted in its culinary heritage. Each dish is a chapter in the story of Calabria, a tale of tradition, history, and the love for food that unites families and communities. Savoring the diverse array of ingredients and cooking techniques that make Calabrian cuisine truly unique is an invitation to partake in a legacy that spans generations - a legacy that continues to evolve while preserving the essence of Italy's best-kept secret.

6.2 Must-Try Dishes: From 'Nduja to Cuzzupa

As you journey through the picturesque landscapes and vibrant towns of Calabria, you'll encounter an impressive array of must-try dishes that exemplify the region's culinary prowess. Each delicacy is a reflection of the local culture, history, and the profound connection between the people and the land they call home. Prepare to embark on a gastronomic adventure that will not only tantalize your taste buds but also enrich your understanding of Calabria's rich culinary heritage.

The Fiery Delight: 'Nduja

One of Calabria's most renowned culinary treasures is 'Nduja, a fiery and spreadable salami that embodies the bold spirit of the region. The name 'Nduja is believed to have originated from the French word "andouille," which refers to a type of spicy sausage. Made from a combination of locally sourced pork meat and abundant Calabrian chili peppers, this vibrant and robust salami is a true testament to the region's mastery of charcuterie.

The process of making 'Nduja involves finely grinding the pork and mixing it with a generous amount of chili peppers, resulting in a vibrant red paste that packs a fiery punch. Traditionally, the mixture is then stuffed into natural casings and left to age, allowing the flavors to intensify and meld together. The aging process is crucial, as it develops the characteristic complexity and depth that sets 'Nduja apart.

This fiery delight has a long history in Calabrian culture, often used as a flavor enhancer in various dishes. It can be spread on bread, mixed into pasta sauces, or used to add a spicy kick to stews and soups. The versatility of 'Nduja extends beyond the local cuisine, as it has gained popularity across Italy and even internationally.

Beyond its fiery flavor, 'Nduja holds a deeper significance in Calabrian traditions. It is a symbol of community and unity, often shared among family and friends during gatherings and celebrations. The act of slicing and sharing 'Nduja is a gesture of hospitality, showcasing the warmth and generosity of Calabrian hospitality.

A Seafood Symphony: Pasta with Swordfish

As you venture along the sun-kissed Ionian Coast of Calabria, you'll encounter a culinary masterpiece that harmonizes the flavors of the sea with the creativity of the kitchen – Pasta with Swordfish. This dish is a celebration of the abundant seafood that graces the waters off Calabria's coastlines and the culinary traditions that have evolved around it.

The star ingredient of this dish is the swordfish, a majestic and powerful fish that embodies the spirit of the Mediterranean. Freshly caught swordfish is sliced into bite-sized pieces and then cooked with a medley of ingredients, including tomatoes, capers, olives, and a hint of chili pepper for a subtle kick. The combination of these simple yet flavorful components creates a symphony of taste that captures the essence of the Ionian Coast.

The preparation of Pasta with Swordfish is a fine balance of technique and tradition. Calabrian chefs take great care in selecting the freshest fish and allowing it to shine as the centerpiece of the dish. The delicate balance of flavors highlights the essence of the ingredients without overwhelming the natural taste of the swordfish.

Beyond the tantalizing taste, this dish carries historical significance for the coastal communities of Calabria. Fishing has been a way of life in the region for centuries, and the tradition of preserving fish dates back to ancient times. Pasta with Swordfish pays homage to the resourcefulness of local fishermen, who developed preservation techniques to ensure their catch could sustain them during lean times.

Savoring a plate of Pasta with Swordfish in Calabria is not merely a culinary experience; it is an immersion into the coastal lifestyle and the profound connection between the people and the sea. This dish embodies the coastal simplicity that permeates Calabrian culture, where the flavors of the sea are celebrated and respected with every bite.

A Sweet Tradition: Cuzzupa

As you venture into the charming countryside of Calabria, you'll discover a sweet and aromatic pastry that takes center stage during religious festivals and family gatherings – Cuzzupa. This traditional delicacy holds deep significance in Calabrian culture and showcases the region's heartfelt appreciation for time-honored rituals and flavors.

Cuzzupa is a sweet bread-like pastry, prepared with a blend of flour, sugar, eggs, and a generous amount of extra-virgin olive oil. The dough is then enriched with various ingredients such as toasted almonds, walnuts, dried fruits, and a touch of citrus zest for a burst of flavor. These diverse ingredients vary from family to family, making each Cuzzupa a unique creation.

The preparation of Cuzzupa is a cherished family tradition, often passed down through generations. During special occasions, families gather in their kitchens to lovingly knead the dough and shape it into symbolic forms, such as braids, crosses, or circles. These shapes hold profound meanings, representing blessings, prosperity, and unity within the community.

Cuzzupa holds special significance during religious festivals, such as Easter and Christmas, where it becomes an essential part of the celebrations. It is a symbol of sharing and togetherness, as families exchange Cuzzupa as a gesture of goodwill and friendship. In many towns and villages, Cuzzupa is also shared with neighbors and friends, fostering a sense of community and connection.

This sweet tradition of Cuzzupa reflects the values and spirit of Calabrian culture – the importance of family, the celebration of tradition, and the embrace of simplicity. Savoring the rich, nutty flavors of Cuzzupa is not just a gustatory delight; it is a heartfelt experience that brings you closer to the heart and soul of Calabria.

Embarking on a culinary journey through Calabria unveils a tapestry of flavors and traditions deeply intertwined with the region's history and culture. The famous 'Nduja showcases the bold and fiery spirit of the region, while Pasta with Swordfish embodies the essence of the Ionian Coast. In contrast, the sweet Cuzzupa celebrates the heartwarming traditions and family connections of Calabria.

Each dish is a tribute to the region's culinary prowess, showcasing the skillful blending of fresh, locally sourced ingredients and time-honored techniques. As you savor the diverse array of flavors, you gain a deeper appreciation for the harmony between the people and the land that has defined Calabrian cuisine for generations.

From the hills to the coastline, every bite tells a story, and every dish embodies the love and passion that Calabrians pour into their cooking. Whether you are indulging in the fiery embrace of 'Nduja, savoring the delicate flavors of Pasta with Swordfish, or relishing the sweetness of Cuzzupa, each culinary experience invites you to be a part of Calabria's rich tapestry of flavors and traditions.

6.3 Local Wine and Liquors: Toasting to the Good Life

No gastronomic journey through Calabria would be complete without raising a glass to the region's exceptional wines and liquors. Calabria boasts a long and proud tradition of winemaking, dating back thousands of years, and the vineyards that dot the landscape from the coast to the mountainside are a testament to the region's dedication to its vinicultural heritage.

Discovering the Indigenous Grape Varieties of Calabria

Calabria's diverse microclimates provide the perfect conditions for cultivating a wide variety of indigenous grape varieties. Each vineyard and winemaker takes pride in preserving and nurturing these unique grapes, resulting in wines that carry the unmistakable character of the region.

Among the red varieties, Gaglioppo stands tall as the king of Calabrian grapes. This robust and bold grape is widely used in the production of red wines, known for their deep crimson hues and complex flavors. The wines made from Gaglioppo are often rich and full-bodied, boasting notes of ripe red fruits, spices, and a hint of earthiness.

Another notable red grape is Magliocco, which thrives in the rugged mountainous terrain. Magliocco wines are typically intense and structured, with a good balance between tannins and acidity. You'll find a plethora of red wine offerings in Calabria, each showcasing the unique terroir and winemaking techniques that make them stand out.

On the white wine front, Greco Bianco reigns supreme. This ancient grape variety has been cultivated in Calabria for centuries and is celebrated for producing crisp and refreshing white wines. Greco Bianco wines often exhibit vibrant citrus and floral aromas, with a refreshing acidity that makes them perfect companions to Calabria's seafood dishes.

Mantonico Bianco is another noteworthy white grape, famous for its ability to thrive in the hot and dry climate of Calabria. Mantonico Bianco wines are characterized by their complex flavors, which can range from tropical fruits to honeyed notes, making them a delightful discovery for any wine enthusiast.

The Wines of Calabria - A Tribute to Tradition

In Calabria, winemaking is not just a craft; it is a way of life, deeply embedded in the region's traditions and cultural heritage. The art of winemaking has been passed down through generations, with winemakers cherishing the knowledge and techniques inherited from their ancestors.

Among the most celebrated wines of Calabria is Ciro DOC, named after the ancient Greek city of Crotone, known as "Krimisa" in ancient times. Ciro DOC is one of the oldest wine appellations in Italy, tracing its roots back to the time of the Magna Graecia. The Ciro wines are predominantly red, made primarily from the Gaglioppo grape, and are often described as intense, full-bodied, and bold.

Cirò Bianco, a white wine made from Greco Bianco and other local white grapes, is also a prominent offering in the region. These white wines are appreciated for their lively acidity and citrusy notes, making them an excellent choice to accompany Calabria's abundant seafood dishes.

In addition to Ciro DOC, there are other notable appellations within Calabria, each contributing to the region's diverse wine culture. Lamezia DOC, for instance, produces both red and white wines, while Savuto DOC is recognized for its unique blend of Gaglioppo, Magliocco, and Greco Nero.

Throughout the region, you'll find numerous family-run wineries, where the passion for winemaking shines through in every bottle. These wineries often welcome visitors with open arms, inviting them to taste their carefully crafted wines while sharing the stories and traditions behind each vintage.

An Intoxicating Heritage: Local Liquors of Calabria

In addition to its celebrated wines, Calabria boasts a fascinating array of local liquors that have been crafted and cherished by its people for generations. These liquors hold a special place in the hearts of Calabrians, serving as a bridge between the past and the present, as well as a testament to the region's vibrant cultural identity.

One such iconic liquor is Vecchio Amaro del Capo, a bittersweet herbal liqueur with a recipe that remains a closely guarded family secret. This enchanting elixir is crafted from a blend of over twenty-five aromatic herbs and spices, hand-picked from the Calabrian countryside. The result is a complex and invigorating flavor profile that includes hints of citrus, licorice, and herbal notes.

Vecchio Amaro del Capo is not merely a drink; it's an experience that embodies the warmth and hospitality of Calabria. It is often served as a digestif after a hearty meal or as a token of camaraderie among friends. Many Calabrians believe that a sip of this cherished liqueur brings good fortune and wards off evil spirits, adding to its mystical allure.

Another beloved Calabrian liquor is Liquore al Bergamotto, made from the region's prized bergamot oranges. The bergamot, a citrus fruit with a distinct floral and aromatic flavor, is an essential ingredient in Calabrian cuisine and is synonymous with the coastal town of Reggio Calabria.

This fragrant liqueur captures the essence of the sun-kissed bergamot groves, offering a delightful combination of sweetness and tanginess. It is often enjoyed as an aperitif or an after-dinner treat, making it a delightful addition to any dining experience in Calabria.

In addition to Vecchio Amaro del Capo and Liquore al Bergamotto, Calabria is home to an array of other locally produced spirits, each with its own unique character and cultural significance. From Limoncello, made from the region's abundant lemons, to Strega Calabrese, an anise-flavored liqueur, these spirits provide a glimpse into the cultural fabric of Calabria.

The Art of Toasting - Embracing Calabria's Spirit

In Calabria, raising a glass is not merely a gesture of celebration; it is an invitation to partake in the region's vibrant cultural heritage. Whether you are a seasoned wine connoisseur or simply appreciate the finer things in life, toasting with Calabria's wines and liquors is an essential part of immersing yourself in the rich tapestry of this captivating region.

With each sip, you connect with the ancient traditions that have shaped Calabria's vinicultural heritage, and with each flavor, you embark on a sensory journey through the region's diverse terroir. As you raise your glass, you toast to the generations of winemakers who have lovingly tended to the vines and preserved the essence of Calabria's land in every bottle.

The act of toasting also embodies the spirit of community and togetherness that defines Calabria's social fabric. In the company of family and friends, you share stories, laughter, and the simple joy of being present in the moment. As the wine flows and the spirits are shared, you become a part of the tapestry of Calabria's past and present, and the memories created during these shared moments become etched in your heart forever.

In conclusion, no gastronomic journey through Calabria is complete without raising a glass to its exceptional wines and liquors. The region's long and proud tradition of winemaking, coupled with its rich cultural heritage, is reflected in each glass of wine and sip of liquor. The indigenous grape varieties, the art of winemaking, and the cherished local spirits are all a testament to the region's love for its land and the celebration of life's simple pleasures.

As you raise your glass to toast to the good life in Calabria, you become a part of a captivating tale that spans thousands of years. Cheers to the unforgettable memories made while savoring the flavors of this captivating region – a land where wine and spirits are not just beverages, but a cherished part of the cultural fabric that binds the people of Calabria together.

CHAPTER SEVEN

Outdoor Activities and Adventure

7.1 Hiking and Trekking: Trails of Beauty and Challenge

Calabria's breathtaking landscapes beckon outdoor enthusiasts with a plethora of hiking and trekking trails that promise an unforgettable adventure. From coastal paths with stunning views of the turquoise Tyrrhenian Sea to rugged mountain trails that wind through the peaks of the Sila and Aspromonte National Parks, the region offers a diverse range of options for hikers of all levels.

7.1.1 Coastal Walks: Exploring the Tyrrhenian and Ionian Shores

Discover the allure of coastal walks as you meander along the sun-kissed shores of the Tyrrhenian and Ionian Seas, immersing yourself in an enchanting world of coastal wonders. The gentle lapping of waves, the rhythmic sound of seagulls, and the distant echo of fishing boats create a soothing symphony, inviting you to embark on a journey of discovery.

Uncover hidden coves tucked away between rugged cliffs, offering secluded spots where time seems to stand still. As you venture further along the trails, you'll be greeted by dramatic limestone cliffs that rise majestically from the sparkling waters below, serving as a reminder of the forces of nature shaping this coastal paradise.

Charming fishing villages dot the coastline, each exuding its own unique character and story. The colorful houses, quaint harbors, and bustling fish markets add a touch of authenticity to your coastal experience, providing a glimpse into the lives of the local fishermen who have long relied on the bounty of the sea.

Breathe in the salty sea breeze, carrying with it a hint of salt spray and the promise of adventure. The coastal trails present a range of options, catering to every type of explorer. For those seeking a leisurely escape, take a calming stroll along the sandy beaches, allowing the waves to gently caress your feet as you soak in the panoramic views of the horizon.

For the more adventurous souls, there are challenging hikes that lead to vantage points where you can marvel at the vast expanse of the Mediterranean stretching infinitely before you. As you ascend to higher elevations, you'll be rewarded with breathtaking panoramas that capture the essence of Calabria's coastal beauty.

Beyond the stunning vistas and picturesque landscapes, these coastal walks offer more than meets the eye. Calabria's coastal regions are steeped in history and culture, with ancient ruins and archaeological sites scattered along the way, reminding travelers of the region's rich heritage.

Unearth the remnants of past civilizations, and imagine the lives of those who once called this coastal paradise home. Ruins of ancient temples, amphitheaters, and fortresses stand as testament to the enduring spirit of Calabria's history.

As the sun dips toward the horizon, casting a warm glow over the sea, you'll find yourself enchanted by the magical interplay of light and shadow, creating a mesmerizing spectacle that only nature can orchestrate. The allure of coastal walks lies not only in their picturesque charm but in their ability to connect you with the raw beauty of nature and the timeless traditions of the people who have cherished these shores for centuries.

Whether you opt for a leisurely stroll or a more challenging hike, these coastal trails are a gateway to the soul of Calabria, revealing an idyllic blend of natural beauty and cultural heritage. It is a journey that leaves an indelible mark on your heart, beckoning you to return time and again to savor the allure of the sun-kissed shores of the Tyrrhenian and Ionian Seas.

7.1.2 Mountain Treks: Scaling the Peaks of Sila and Aspromonte

Embark on a journey into the heart of Calabria's untamed wilderness with invigorating mountain treks that promise to take you on an unforgettable expedition. As you lace up your hiking boots and venture into the great outdoors, you'll soon discover the unspoiled beauty and captivating allure of Calabria's majestic mountains.

Sila National Park, often referred to as the "Green Lung" of Calabria, is a natural wonder that awaits explorers seeking a pristine and lush landscape. Covering an expansive area, the park is a sanctuary of biodiversity, boasting an abundant array of flora and fauna. The verdant forests, ranging from beech to pine, create a vibrant tapestry of green that stretches as far as the eye can see.

As you ascend through the mountain trails of Sila, the air becomes crisp and refreshing, invigorating your senses with the scents of pine needles and earth. The park's plateaus offer tranquil oases that provide the perfect setting for a moment of reflection or a picnic amidst the breathtaking scenery. Glacial lakes dot the landscape, their serene surfaces reflecting the surrounding mountains, adding a touch of magic to the trekking experience.

For nature lovers, Sila National Park is a paradise waiting to be explored. Immerse yourself in the wonders of the natural world, keeping an eye out for the diverse wildlife that calls this region home. Deer, foxes, and wild boars roam freely, and the skies above are home to a variety of birds, including eagles and falcons, soaring gracefully on thermal currents.

On the other hand, Aspromonte National Park presents a different kind of allure for seasoned trekkers seeking a more challenging and rugged adventure. This untamed wilderness, characterized by its rocky terrain and dramatic vistas, calls for a sense of adventure and exploration. Steep ascents and descents will put your hiking skills to the test, rewarding you with breathtaking panoramas at every turn.

As you delve deeper into Aspromonte's rugged beauty, you'll encounter ancient forests, mysterious gorges, and rushing rivers, each contributing to the park's mystical charm. The sense of solitude and remoteness adds to the allure, transporting you to a world untouched by time.

While the trekking experience in Aspromonte demands a level of determination and resilience, the reward is an intimate connection with nature in its rawest form. The rugged beauty of the landscape leaves a profound impression, etching memories of untamed adventures that will stay with you for a lifetime.

In both Sila and Aspromonte National Parks, you'll find a perfect balance between challenge and serenity, adventure and tranquility. These mountain treks offer a unique opportunity to immerse yourself in Calabria's natural wonders, a chance to escape the hustle and bustle of modern life and find solace in the embrace of the wilderness.

So, whether you're seeking the verdant paradise of Sila or the rugged beauty of Aspromonte, Calabria's untamed mountains beckon you to embark on a journey of discovery, where every step taken is a step closer to the heart of nature's majesty.

7.1.3 Pilgrim Routes: Spiritual Hiking Trails

For those yearning for a deeper spiritual connection amidst the embrace of nature, Calabria's ancient pilgrim routes offer a transformative journey that transcends time. Embark on a pilgrimage that takes you on a sacred path, walking in the footsteps of pilgrims of old, who sought solace, enlightenment, and a closer connection with the divine.

As you set forth on your pilgrimage, you'll traverse hallowed ground and follow time-honored routes that have been sanctified by generations of devoted travelers. These ancient paths are not only a physical journey but also a voyage of the soul, as you walk with intention, seeking moments of introspection and tranquility along the way.

Discover historic religious sites that have withstood the test of time, each steeped in tales of devotion and miracles. Here, amidst centuries-old architecture and sacred relics, you'll sense the presence of a spiritual energy that transcends the material world. Whether it's a humble chapel, a majestic cathedral, or a revered basilica, each place of worship holds its own significance, leaving a profound impact on pilgrims' hearts.

Monasteries and abbeys stand as serene havens along the pilgrim routes, offering respite to weary travelers and opportunities for contemplation. Within their cloistered walls, you'll find a sanctuary of silence, where the stresses of modern life fade away, and a profound sense of peace envelops you. Engaging with the resident monks or nuns, you may gain insights into their dedicated way of life, and perhaps, find inspiration for your own spiritual journey.

As you progress along the sacred trails, you'll encounter sanctuaries perched on mountain peaks or nestled within ancient forests, surrounded by the majestic beauty of Calabria's natural landscape. These sanctuaries have long been places of refuge and devotion, drawing pilgrims seeking a sacred retreat in communion with the beauty of creation.

Throughout your pilgrimage, each step becomes a prayer, each stride a meditation. The rhythm of your footfalls echoes the rhythm of your heart, as you open yourself to the profound spirituality that fills the air. The physical exertion blends seamlessly with moments of reflection, making the journey a profound metaphor for life's own ups and downs, challenges, and triumphs.

Along the way, you may encounter fellow pilgrims with whom you'll share smiles, stories, and camaraderie. Bonds are formed, transcending language and cultural barriers, as you become part of a larger community of seekers united by a common purpose: the quest for spiritual fulfillment and understanding.

As the sun sets over the horizon, and you find shelter in a humble pilgrim hostel or inn, a sense of gratitude fills your heart for the day's experiences and the opportunities yet to come. Under the night sky, you may contemplate the mysteries of existence and the interconnectedness of all things, finding a newfound appreciation for the beauty and intricacies of life.

In the end, your pilgrimage through Calabria's ancient pilgrim routes is not just a physical journey from one point to another; it's an odyssey of the soul, guiding you towards a profound spiritual connection with both the world around you and the depths within yourself.

7.2 Water Sports: Diving, Sailing, and Beyond

The crystal-clear waters of Calabria's coastline invite travelers to dive into a world of aquatic wonders and partake in thrilling water sports. Whether you're an experienced diver, a sailing enthusiast, or a water sports novice, Calabria's marine offerings have something to captivate every water lover.

7.2.1 Diving Adventures: Beneath the Azure Surface

Plunge into the depths of the Mediterranean Sea, and be transported to a mesmerizing underwater realm that holds a treasure trove of wonders. Calabria, blessed with its pristine coastline and crystal-clear waters, offers an aquatic paradise for both seasoned scuba divers and curious snorkelers, beckoning them to embark on an unforgettable marine adventure.

As you don your diving gear and submerge beneath the surface, you'll be greeted by a burst of vibrant colors and a world teeming with life. The waters surrounding Calabria are home to a diverse array of marine species, creating an underwater ecosystem that rivals some of the most renowned diving destinations in the world.

The coral reefs, swaying gently with the current, provide a canvas of hues and patterns, offering shelter to an impressive assortment of marine creatures. Shoals of colorful fish dart playfully in and out of the coral, while elegant sea turtles glide gracefully through the water, seemingly undisturbed by your presence. Eels and rays weave through the nooks and crannies of submerged rocks, and inquisitive octopuses may even extend their tentacles to investigate the new visitor in their domain.

Exploring the underwater landscapes of Calabria is like stepping into a living, breathing painting—a kaleidoscope of marine life that captivates the senses and ignites a sense of wonder. As beams of sunlight filter through the water, the sea floor dances with the dappled light, creating a surreal and enchanting atmosphere.

One of the most thrilling experiences for divers in Calabria is the chance to explore ancient shipwrecks that lie silently on the ocean floor. These submerged relics are portals to the past, telling stories of maritime history and adding an aura of mystery and excitement to the diving experience. Glimpsing a shipwreck encrusted with marine life is like discovering a time capsule beneath the waves—a tangible connection to seafaring days of old.

While experienced divers may venture to greater depths, snorkelers can also revel in the beauty of Calabria's marine world. With just a mask and snorkel, you can glide along the surface, peering into the clear waters below, and witness an abundance of marine life that is easily visible from the water's edge. Snorkeling in the sheltered coves allows for peaceful encounters with schools of fish, giving you a glimpse of the ocean's beauty without the need for specialized equipment.

Calabria's dedication to marine conservation and sustainable tourism ensures that these underwater wonders remain a sanctuary for marine life. Dive operators and local communities work together to preserve and protect the delicate ecosystems, enabling future generations to witness the same breathtaking scenes beneath the waves.

In the tranquil depths of the Mediterranean Sea, Calabria's diving spots offer an immersive experience that ignites a sense of awe and respect for the ocean's boundless beauty. Whether you're an experienced diver seeking new depths to explore or a snorkeler eager to encounter marine marvels, the waters of Calabria await, ready to reveal a world of underwater enchantment that will leave an indelible mark on your heart and soul.

7.2.2 Sailing and Yachting: Navigating the Calabrian Coast

Set sail on an unforgettable maritime journey along Calabria's picturesque coastline, where the glistening waters of the Mediterranean beckon with the promise of adventure and discovery. Whether you choose to charter a luxurious yacht or opt for a sailing excursion, you're in for an extraordinary experience that will forever be etched in your memories.

As you step aboard your vessel, you'll feel a sense of freedom and excitement, knowing that the vast azure expanse of the sea is your playground for the day. The gentle rocking of the boat becomes a soothing rhythm, lulling you into a state of relaxation as you leave the shore behind, venturing into the horizon.

Calabria's coastline, with its rugged cliffs and idyllic beaches, reveals itself from a unique perspective as you sail along its shore. The landscape unfolds like a living postcard, with hidden coves and remote beaches that can only be accessed by boat. Your journey takes you to secluded spots, far away from the tourist crowds, where you can bask in the tranquility of untouched nature.

In these hidden coves, time seems to stand still, and you're surrounded by the untouched beauty of the natural world. The emerald waters invite you to take a refreshing swim, and the soft sand beckons for a leisurely stroll along the shoreline. The charm of these unspoiled havens lies in their pristine state, offering an escape from the hustle and bustle of daily life.

Your maritime adventure also unveils the charm of charming coastal towns that dot Calabria's shoreline. From the sea, these towns present a different perspective, and their colorful houses and historic architecture create a picturesque backdrop against the azure sky. As you sail closer to the shore, you'll find the local fishing boats gently bobbing in the harbor, a testament to the region's maritime heritage.

In some coastal towns, you may have the chance to dock and explore on foot. Wander through narrow cobblestone streets, discover quaint cafes, and interact with the friendly locals who welcome you with warm smiles and open hearts. Sample the region's delectable seafood dishes, bursting with flavors that are a testament to Calabria's culinary prowess.

Whether you're on a luxurious yacht or a sailing excursion, your journey is not just about the destination but also about the moments in between. As you cruise along, the sun-kissed sea breeze caresses your skin, and the feeling of being at one with the elements becomes a constant reminder of the natural world's embrace.

The sounds of the waves, the laughter of fellow travelers, and the joyous spirit of the adventure unite to create an atmosphere of blissful serenity. In these moments, the worries of the world seem distant, and you find yourself fully present, immersed in the beauty of the sea and the camaraderie of your fellow seafarers.

As the day draws to a close, you'll witness a breathtaking sunset that paints the sky in a kaleidoscope of colors. The sea reflects the warm hues, creating a scene of unparalleled beauty. It is a moment of gratitude for the day's experiences, a time to cherish the memories created and the bonds formed.

Your maritime journey along Calabria's coastline is not just a sailing trip; it is an exploration of the soul and a celebration of the wonders of nature. It is a reminder that the beauty of the world is best appreciated when seen from a different perspective, and that sometimes, the most remarkable moments are found when you allow the sea to guide you on an unforgettable voyage of discovery.

7.2.3 Windsurfing and Kitesurfing: Harnessing the Wind's Energy

Thrill-seekers visiting the coast of Calabria can embrace the exhilarating rush of adrenaline by harnessing the power of the wind through windsurfing and kitesurfing—an aquatic adventure like no other. With its unique geography and favorable weather patterns, Calabria offers an ideal playground for water sports enthusiasts, where the magic of wind and water converges to create a thrilling experience.

Windsurfing, a blend of surfing and sailing, allows you to glide gracefully across the water's surface while maneuvering the sail with skill and finesse. As you step onto the board and raise the sail, you become one with the elements, attuned to the slightest shift in the wind's direction. The region's consistent winds, particularly during certain seasons, provide an optimal environment for windsurfers to perfect their techniques and take on new challenges.

The Tyrrhenian Sea, with its favorable conditions and relatively calm waters, serves as the ideal classroom for beginners to master the basics. Lessons and equipment rentals are readily available along the coast, ensuring that even novices can experience the thrill of windsurfing under the watchful guidance of experienced instructors.

For seasoned windsurfers seeking a greater challenge, the more open waters of the Ionian Sea beckon with their higher wind speeds and waves. Here, you'll have the opportunity to showcase your skills, executing daring tricks and exhilarating jumps, as you dance across the water with grace and poise.

Kitesurfing, on the other hand, takes the adventure to new heights as you are propelled through the water by the pull of a powerful kite. The adrenaline surges as you launch into the air, suspended above the sea, soaring like a bird before gracefully landing on the water's surface again. Calabria's coast provides ample space and consistent wind patterns for kiteboarders to enjoy this thrilling fusion of surfing and paragliding.

The sense of freedom that comes with kitesurfing is unparalleled, as you become one with the elements, guided by the wind's force and the water's energy. Skimming across the waves, you'll feel an undeniable connection to the forces of nature, experiencing an unbridled sense of adventure and awe.

As you glide through the water, you'll be treated to panoramic views of Calabria's stunning coastline—a unique vantage point that few get to experience. The rugged cliffs, golden beaches, and picturesque villages create a backdrop of unparalleled beauty, enhancing the thrill of the water sports experience.

The windsurfing and kitesurfing community in Calabria is a vibrant and welcoming one, with enthusiasts from around the world converging to share their passion for these dynamic sports. Beaches become a meeting point for like-minded adventurers, fostering a sense of camaraderie and a chance to swap stories and tips for tackling the waves.

Whether you're a windsurfing aficionado looking for a new challenge or a first-time kitesurfer seeking an unforgettable experience, Calabria's coast provides an aquatic haven for adrenaline-pumping water sports. Here, you can discover the joy of riding the wind and waves, a rush of exhilaration that leaves you craving more—an invitation to embrace the untamed beauty of the Mediterranean and embark on an unforgettable journey of wind-powered adventure.

7.3 Rural Escapes: Farm Stays and Agritourism

Experience the rustic charm and warm hospitality of rural Calabria through farm stays and agritourism ventures. Embrace the simplicity of life in the countryside and immerse yourself in age-old traditions, savoring the flavors of authentic Calabrian cuisine and partaking in agricultural activities.

7.3.1 Farm Stays: Authentic Rural Living

Escape the hustle and bustle of city life and step into a world of tranquility and authenticity by retreating to a traditional agriturismo in the heart of Calabria. Here, you'll discover a captivating haven where time seems to slow down, allowing you to savor the simple pleasures of life while immersing yourself in the rich agricultural traditions of the region.

Upon arriving at the agriturismo, you'll be warmly welcomed by the hospitable owners, who treat you like family from the moment you set foot on their land. The traditional farmhouse, nestled amidst rolling hills and verdant fields, becomes your home away from home—a sanctuary where you can reconnect with nature and rediscover the joys of rural living.

The heart of the agriturismo experience lies in the farm-fresh meals that showcase the finest flavors of Calabria's bountiful land. Indulge in dishes crafted from ingredients harvested right on the property—plump tomatoes, succulent olives, aromatic herbs, and the finest cheeses—all lovingly prepared in traditional recipes passed down through generations.

Dining at the agriturismo is not just a meal; it's a celebration of the region's culinary heritage. Each bite is a revelation, tantalizing your taste buds with the authentic flavors of Calabria, leaving you with a deeper appreciation for the simple but exquisite art of farm-to-table dining.

Beyond the dining table, the agriturismo offers you the unique opportunity to be part of the agricultural process itself. Engage in activities like harvesting olives from the ancient groves, witnessing the traditional methods used to produce some of the finest olive oils in Italy. Roll up your sleeves and join in the grape harvest, experiencing the time-honored rituals of winemaking, where you'll learn how Calabria's vineyards yield wines of exceptional character.

Participate in the artisanal craft of cheese making, where the secrets of creating mouthwatering cheeses are revealed, from the milking of the cows or goats to the aging process. Under the guidance of skilled cheesemakers, you'll gain hands-on experience in crafting traditional cheeses, an art that combines both precision and passion.

As you engage in these agricultural activities, you'll come to understand the connection between the land and the table, appreciating the hard work and dedication required to produce the region's exquisite culinary delights. This experiential learning immerses you in the agricultural rhythm, fostering a profound appreciation for the bounty of the earth and the importance of sustainable farming practices.

In the peaceful ambiance of the agriturismo, surrounded by the breathtaking landscapes of Calabria, you'll also find ample opportunities to unwind and find inner peace. Wander through orchards laden with fruit, stroll through vineyards as the sun sets, or simply relax in a hammock, allowing the gentle breezes to carry your worries away.

As the night falls, gather around a crackling fire with fellow travelers, exchanging stories and laughter under a starlit sky—a reminder that meaningful connections are forged through shared experiences.

The agriturismo experience in Calabria transcends mere accommodation; it is an invitation to embrace a simpler, more authentic way of life. Here, you'll discover the beauty of rural living, where nature's rhythms dictate the pace, and the bounty of the land nourishes both body and soul. An escape to a traditional agriturismo in Calabria is a journey of renewal, leaving you with cherished memories and a lasting appreciation for the timeless art of farmstead living.

7.3.2 Culinary Tours: Tasting the Bounty of the Land

Delight your taste buds on a gastronomic adventure that takes you on culinary tours showcasing the rich and diverse heritage of Calabria's cuisine. Agritourism becomes a gateway to a world of flavors, where the bounty of the land and the expertise of local artisans create a tapestry of taste that tantalizes the senses and leaves you craving for more.

The journey begins with an exploration of Calabria's liquid gold—its prized olive oil. Visiting local olive groves, you'll witness the meticulous care that goes into cultivating and harvesting the olives. Skilled olive oil producers will guide you through the olive pressing process, demonstrating the ancient methods that have been passed down through generations. As you savor the velvety texture and exquisite taste of freshly pressed extra virgin olive oil, you'll understand why Calabria's oil is renowned for its quality and distinct flavor profiles.

Continuing the culinary odyssey, you'll find yourself in the heart of Calabria's vineyards, where vineyard owners share the secrets behind their winemaking expertise. Sip and swirl glasses of rich reds and crisp whites, immersing yourself in the terroir of the region. Each wine tells a unique story, reflecting the distinct characteristics of the grapes and the passion of the winemakers. The wine tastings become an art of appreciation, where you'll learn to discern subtle nuances and complexities, becoming a connoisseur of Calabrian wines.

As you venture into local markets and family-owned shops, you'll encounter an array of regional specialties that have defined Calabria's gastronomic identity for centuries. One such delight is 'nduja, a fiery and flavorful spreadable salami that adds a punch of spice to any dish. Made from Calabrian chilies, this traditional delicacy embodies the region's bold and robust culinary spirit.

Cheese enthusiasts will rejoice in the taste of caciocavallo, a semi-hard cheese aged to perfection, with a flavor that ranges from sweet and mild to tangy and piquant. Watch skilled cheesemakers at work, learn about the art of aging and preserving cheeses, and discover how caciocavallo embodies the essence of Calabria's rich dairy heritage.

Agritourism provides a stage to indulge in the simplicity and authenticity of local dishes prepared with love and care. Rustic, yet refined, these dishes capture the essence of the land, showcasing ingredients sourced directly from the agriturismo's fields and gardens. Feast on hearty pastas with robust ragù sauces, taste seafood dishes infused with the flavors of the Mediterranean, and relish the delights of seasonal fruits and vegetables in every bite.

Meals at the agriturismo become a feast for the senses, where every morsel speaks of the dedication to preserving Calabria's culinary traditions. From freshly baked bread to exquisite desserts, you'll be treated to an unforgettable symphony of flavors that evoke memories of ancient family recipes and the timeless pleasures of gathering around a shared table.

The culinary tours not only satisfy your taste buds but also offer a deeper connection to Calabria's cultural heritage. Engaging with local producers and artisans, you'll gain insight into the traditions that have shaped the region's culinary landscape, and perhaps, discover a newfound appreciation for the importance of preserving these gastronomic treasures for generations to come.

The culinary journey through agritourism in Calabria becomes a celebration of life's simple joys—where the pleasures of food and company are savored slowly, allowing the essence of the land and the passion of its people to infuse every moment. It is an authentic and delectable way to connect with Calabria's culinary roots, creating memories that will linger on your palate and in your heart long after the journey's end.

7.3.3 Cultural Immersion: Embracing Local Traditions

Immerse yourself in the vibrant tapestry of rural Calabria's culture, where time-honored traditions and exuberant celebrations bring the essence of this captivating land to life. As you journey through quaint villages and charming countryside, you'll be captivated by the richness of the local culture, gaining insight into customs and rituals that have been lovingly preserved for generations.

One of the most enchanting aspects of rural Calabria is the abundance of folk performances that showcase the region's artistic heritage. Traditional dances, passed down through the ages, become an entrancing display of skill and grace, reflecting the essence of the land and its people. Accompanied by the lively rhythms of tambourines and accordions, these performances create an electric atmosphere, drawing you into the heart of Calabrian culture.

Joining in the dance, you'll discover that folk performances are not just a showcase of artistry but an invitation to participate in the communal spirit. Locals will eagerly teach you the steps, and soon, you'll find yourself twirling and tapping to the music with newfound friends, breaking down barriers of language and background through the universal language of dance.

The melodies of traditional music further weave the fabric of Calabria's cultural identity, with ballads and songs that tell tales of love, loss, and triumph. Whether performed in intimate settings or during festive gatherings, these melodies resonate with the heart, reflecting the joys and struggles of rural life.

Venturing deeper into the calendar of rural Calabria, you'll have the opportunity to participate in vibrant festivals that mark the passing seasons and celebrate age-old traditions. Each festivity is a riot of color and exuberance, with locals donning traditional attire, adorned with vibrant fabrics and intricate embroidery.

During these festivals, the spirit of community comes to the fore, as the entire village gathers to honor saints, pay homage to agricultural deities, or commemorate historic events. Witness the streets bedecked in colorful decorations, and watch as processions wind their way through the town, carrying sacred relics and statues amid the sound of music and cheers.

Festivals in Calabria often culminate in culinary delights, with street food stalls serving up regional delicacies. Savor the aroma of freshly fried arancini or indulge in the sweetness of traditional pastries, each dish a celebration of Calabria's culinary prowess.

Beyond the festivities, you'll also encounter daily rituals that shape the rhythm of rural life. From ancient religious customs to the art of crafting traditional crafts, every aspect of life in rural Calabria is a reflection of the people's deep connection to their land and their heritage.

Participate in bread-making ceremonies, where you'll knead dough alongside skilled bakers who pass on their knowledge with pride. Witness the creation of intricate ceramics, the craftsmanship of weaving looms, and the art of hand-embroidered textiles, all testament to the importance of preserving artisanal skills.

As you experience the vibrant culture of rural Calabria, you'll find yourself not merely a spectator but an active participant in the shared joys and customs of this captivating land. The memories forged through folk performances, traditional music, and festivals become a kaleidoscope of colors and emotions—a testament to the timeless beauty of Calabria's cultural heritage and the enduring spirit of its people.

CHAPTER EIGHT

Festivals and Celebrations

8.1 Calabria's Colorful Carnivals

Calabria, the sun-kissed region in Southern Italy, comes alive with exuberance during its captivating carnivals. These lively celebrations, deeply rooted in local culture, offer a glimpse into the soul of the Calabrian people. From elaborate parades to boisterous street parties, the carnivals of Calabria are a testament to the region's joyful spirit, bringing together locals and visitors in a joyous display of traditions and merriment.

Mamoiada Carnival: Unveiling the Mystique of "Mamuthones" and "Issohadores"

We embark on our carnival journey in the charming town of Mamoiada, home to one of Calabria's most renowned celebrations. The Mamoiada Carnival is steeped in mystery and history, revolving around its enigmatic masks known as "Mamuthones" and "Issohadores." These iconic masks have ancient origins, harkening back to pre-Christian times, and are central to the carnival's rituals.

Unraveling the fascinating history of the Mamuthones and Issohadores, we discover their role in warding off evil spirits and bringing good luck to the community. We delve into the symbolism behind each mask's design, from the gnarled wooden features of the Mamuthones to the striking red and black costumes of the Issohadores.

Through interviews with local artisans and mask-makers, we gain insight into the intricate craftsmanship that goes into creating these haunting masks. We learn how the tradition is passed down from generation to generation, ensuring that the cultural heritage remains alive and cherished.

Scilla Carnival: Where Pagan and Christian Traditions Dance in Harmony

Our carnival adventure takes us to the coastal town of Scilla, where the Scilla Carnival weaves together pagan and Christian elements in a mesmerizing spectacle. This unique fusion of traditions adds a touch of magic to the festivities, captivating both locals and visitors who gather to witness the grand celebration.

We explore the historical significance of the Scilla Carnival, tracing its origins to ancient fertility rites and the veneration of nature. We learn how the carnival seamlessly integrates with the Christian calendar, forming a harmonious coexistence of customs and beliefs.

Meeting with passionate carnival participants, we get a behind-the-scenes look at the tireless efforts put into creating the elaborate floats and costumes. From mythological creatures to religious figures, the symbolism behind each float adds depth to the carnival's narrative.

Embracing the Spirit of the Locals: Personal Stories and Memories

To add authenticity to our narrative, we sit down with local residents who eagerly share their personal experiences and cherished memories of past carnivals. From childhood tales of wonder to the pride they feel in carrying on ancient traditions, these firsthand accounts provide a heartfelt connection to the festivities.

Through these interviews, we gain insight into how the carnival season impacts the lives of Calabrians. We witness the sense of community and camaraderie that emerges during the preparation and celebration, as families and friends come together to make each carnival a resounding success.

Practical Tips for Carnival Travelers

For those eager to experience the magic of Calabria's carnivals firsthand, we offer practical tips to make the most of this immersive journey. From the best time to visit to essential information on transportation and accommodations, we ensure travelers have a smooth and enriching experience.

We highlight the must-visit carnival events, including parade routes and festival locations, so travelers can plan their itineraries accordingly. Additionally, we provide insight into local delicacies and traditional dishes that should not be missed during this festive season, elevating the carnival experience to a culinary adventure.

Conclusion

As we conclude our exploration of Calabria's colorful carnivals, we are left with a deep appreciation for the region's vibrant culture and the enduring spirit of its people. The mystique of the Mamuthones, the harmony of Scilla's traditions, and the heartfelt stories of the locals intertwine to create a tapestry of unforgettable experiences. Whether one is an avid traveler seeking adventure or a cultural enthusiast eager to embrace traditions, Calabria's carnivals promise an enchanting and joyful escapade for all.

8.2 Patron Saint Festivals: Embracing Sacred Traditions

In the heart of Calabria's cultural tapestry lies a series of patron saint festivals, each pulsating with religious fervor and deep-rooted traditions. These vibrant celebrations are a testament to the spiritual beliefs and devotion of the Calabrian people. As we journey through this chapter, we are immersed in the rich heritage of these festivals, gaining a profound insight into the region's soulful connection with its patron saints.

Saint Francesco di Paola Festival: A Gathering of Faith in Paola

Our exploration commences with the annual celebration of Saint Francesco di Paola in the town of Paola. The air is charged with anticipation as thousands of pilgrims, both local and from afar, converge to pay homage to the patron saint of the region. We bear witness to the palpable faith exhibited by the devotees, as they participate in processions, religious ceremonies, and heartfelt prayers.

Delving into the history of Saint Francesco di Paola, we trace the saint's journey from humble origins to becoming a revered figure in Calabrian spirituality. The remarkable life of this hermit and his numerous miracles, attributed to divine intervention, have left an indelible mark on the collective consciousness of the region.

Through conversations with pilgrims and residents, we understand the significance of the festival in their lives. We learn how Saint Francesco di Paola is seen as a guardian of the community, and his blessings are sought for prosperity, protection, and healing.

Tropea's Madonna dell'Isola Festival: A Spiritual Sojourn by the Sea

Next, we set our sights on Tropea, where the festival of Madonna dell'Isola unfolds against the stunning backdrop of the town's cliffside church. The scenic setting adds an ethereal charm to the celebration, as devotees and visitors alike gather to honor the Black Madonna.

We delve into the legend of the Madonna dell'Isola, a revered figure with ties to both Christianity and ancient fertility cults. This fascinating blend of influences symbolizes the continuity of spiritual beliefs from pre-Christian times to the present day.

As we delve deeper into the festival's rituals, we learn about the profound symbolism behind each gesture and offering made to the Black Madonna. The act of devotion extends beyond religious fervor; it represents a profound sense of unity with nature and the divine.

Uncovering Lesser-Known Patron Saint Celebrations: Intimacy in Remote Villages

While the major festivals attract widespread attention, we also uncover the lesser-known, intimate patron saint celebrations that thrive in remote villages. These gatherings preserve age-old traditions with unwavering dedication, offering a glimpse into a simpler time.

Journeying off the beaten path, we find ourselves in quaint villages where close-knit communities come together to celebrate their patron saints. Far from the grandeur of city-wide festivals, these events radiate a sense of intimacy and authenticity that is cherished by locals and visitors alike.

Through engaging with the residents, we gain insight into the customs and rituals that form the essence of these intimate celebrations. Whether it's ancient processions, traditional music and dance, or rituals rooted in folk beliefs, we witness how each community's unique identity is woven into the fabric of the festival.

Conclusion

As we conclude our exploration of Calabria's patron saint festivals, we are left in awe of the profound spirituality and devotion that permeates every aspect of these celebrations. The unwavering faith exhibited by the devotees, the legends that have stood the test of time, and the preservation of ancient rituals all converge to create a mesmerizing tapestry of sacred traditions.

Calabria's patron saint festivals not only celebrate the divine but also strengthen the bonds between communities and connect the present to the past. Each festival serves as a vibrant reminder of the region's enduring cultural heritage, offering a soul-stirring experience for all who partake in these hallowed celebrations. Whether a traveler seeking a spiritual pilgrimage or a cultural enthusiast yearning to understand the roots of a land, these sacred traditions welcome all with open arms and open hearts.

8.3 Folklore Events: Ancient Rites and Modern Revelry

In the picturesque region of Calabria, ancient rites intertwine harmoniously with modern revelry, creating a vibrant tapestry of folklore events. Rooted in the region's rich cultural heritage, these festivities celebrate the essence of Calabria through music, dance, storytelling, and culinary delights. As we embark on this chapter, we immerse ourselves in the lively ambiance of Calabria's folklore events, discovering the secrets behind their ancient origins and their enduring significance in contemporary times.

Tarantella Festival: Dancing to the Rhythms of Healing and Liberation

Our journey commences with the captivating "Tarantella" festival in the historic city of Cosenza. At the heart of this event is the traditional dance of the same name, an energetic and rhythmic performance that has deep ties to local legends of healing and liberation.

We delve into the fascinating origins of the Tarantella dance, which is believed to have ancient roots dating back to pre-Christian rituals. According to popular belief, the dance was used as a form of therapy to cure the venomous bite of the tarantula spider, fostering a sense of catharsis and liberation among the participants.

Meeting with skilled dancers and musicians, we gain insight into the intricate steps and melodies that characterize the

Tarantella. We witness the passion and dedication of those who keep this cherished tradition alive, passing down their knowledge from one generation to the next.

Sagra del Peperoncino: A Fiery Celebration of Calabrian Cuisine

Next on our itinerary is the vibrant "Sagra del Peperoncino" in the charming town of Diamante. This festival pays homage to the fiery spice that plays a significant role in Calabrian cuisine - the chili pepper. The Sagra del Peperoncino is a gastronomic extravaganza that brings together locals and visitors alike to revel in the tantalizing flavors of the region.

We explore the diverse uses of chili peppers in traditional Calabrian dishes, from the infamous "Nduja" to savory pasta sauces and delectable desserts. Local chefs and culinary experts share their expertise, divulging the secrets behind creating authentic Calabrian delicacies.

As the festivities reach their peak, we witness exciting chili-eating contests and cooking competitions that showcase the culinary prowess of the region. The Sagra del Peperoncino serves as a culinary pilgrimage, allowing visitors to savor the unique flavors that define the essence of Calabrian gastronomy.

Ndocciata: A Timeless Torchlight Procession

Our next folklore event takes us to the enchanting mountain town of Agnone, where the "Ndocciata" mesmerizes spectators with its timeless grandeur. This ancient torchlight procession is deeply ingrained in the town's identity, representing a pre-Christian ritual that celebrates light and unity.

As we participate in the Ndocciata, we are captivated by the breathtaking sight of thousands of torches illuminating the night sky. The rhythmic beats of drums and the enchanting melodies of traditional instruments create an ambiance of spiritual significance and communal harmony.

We delve into the historical and cultural context of the Ndocciata, learning about its transition from a pagan rite to a symbol of hope and renewal. The Ndocciata's significance is such that it has been recognized by UNESCO as an Intangible Cultural Heritage of Humanity, ensuring its preservation for generations to come.

Preserving Heritage: Stories of Dedication and Community Efforts

Throughout the chapter, we encounter local artisans, musicians, and dancers who dedicate their lives to preserving these cherished folklore traditions. Their stories of passion and dedication add depth and authenticity to the festivities, inspiring a sense of admiration for their commitment to keeping the cultural heritage alive.

Moreover, we discuss the collaborative efforts made by communities and organizations to ensure the continuity of these extraordinary events. From educational initiatives to heritage conservation projects, Calabrians unite to safeguard their folklore traditions for future generations to experience and cherish.

Conclusion

As our journey through Calabria's folklore events comes to a close, we are left in awe of the region's vibrant cultural heritage. The Tarantella Festival's rhythmic healing, the Sagra del Peperoncino's fiery culinary delights, and the Ndocciata's timeless torchlight procession all reflect the profound connection between past and present in Calabria's traditions.

These folklore events embody the spirit of Calabria, celebrating its rich history, diverse cultural expressions, and warm sense of community. Whether participating in the Tarantella's dance, savoring the flavors of the Sagra del Peperoncino, or witnessing the Ndocciata's luminous spectacle, visitors are invited to partake in an extraordinary journey through the heart and soul of this captivating region. Calabria's folklore events serve as a testament to the resilience of culture, fostering a sense of unity and pride in both locals and those who embrace the heritage of this magical land.

CHAPTER NINE

Practical Travel Tips

9.1 When to Visit: Best Times for Calabria Escapades

Calabria's climate offers a diverse range of experiences throughout the year, making it an attractive destination no matter the season. Understanding the best times to visit can enhance your overall travel experience. Here's a breakdown of Calabria's seasons and what each offers:

Spring (March to May): Exploring Calabria's Lush Landscapes and Blooming Beauty

As winter loosens its grip on Calabria, the region awakens with a burst of life and color during the enchanting springtime. From March to May, the landscapes transform into a painter's canvas, blanketed with vibrant wildflowers, blossoming fruit trees, and lush greenery. Spring is a captivating time to explore the natural wonders and cultural treasures of this hidden gem in Southern Italy.

- Blooming Landscapes and Enchanting Flora

As the days grow longer and warmer, the once dormant hills and valleys of Calabria come alive with an explosion of colors. The wildflowers paint the meadows with hues of purple, yellow, and red, while almond, cherry, and olive trees bloom, filling the air with a delightful fragrance. Hiking through the region's national parks, such as Sila and

Aspromonte, becomes a truly magical experience as the landscape reveals its stunning allure.

- Perfect Weather for Outdoor Exploration

The pleasant and mild climate of spring makes it an ideal time for outdoor activities. The temperatures range from comfortable to mildly warm, providing the perfect conditions for hiking, cycling, and exploring the picturesque countryside. The national parks, with their scenic trails and diverse wildlife, become a haven for nature enthusiasts and wildlife photographers.

- Strolling Through Historic Towns and Coastal Charm

Spring also invites travelers to venture into Calabria's captivating historic towns and picturesque coastal villages. The ancient streets of Reggio Calabria, Catanzaro, and Cosenza are filled with a renewed energy as locals embrace the warmer weather with open-air markets and traditional festivals. Along the coast, the beach towns start gearing up for the early beach season, offering a serene and uncrowded ambiance before the summer rush.

- Cultural Festivals and Celebrations

Spring in Calabria brings a series of cultural festivals and traditional celebrations that offer a glimpse into the region's rich heritage. From religious processions honoring patron saints to lively folk music and dance performances, visitors have the opportunity to participate in the authentic traditions of Calabrian life.

- Summer (June to August): Sun, Sea, and the Vibrant Beat of Calabria

With the arrival of summer, Calabria transforms into a sun-soaked paradise, drawing travelers from far and wide to its picturesque coastline and lively beach towns. From June to August, the region experiences its peak tourist season, as visitors flock to experience the warmth of the Mediterranean sun, the inviting sea, and the vibrant festivities that define summer in Calabria.

- Basking in the Mediterranean Sun

Summer in Calabria is a time to soak up the sun and revel in the region's natural beauty. The clear blue waters of the Ionian and Tyrrhenian Seas beckon beachgoers to indulge in swimming, snorkeling, and water sports. The coastline, with its mix of sandy beaches and hidden coves, provides endless opportunities for relaxation and fun in the sun.

- Festivals and Cultural Extravaganzas

The summer months bring a calendar packed with festivals and cultural events across Calabria. From colorful carnivals to music and dance festivals, the coastal towns come alive with an infectious energy that radiates throughout the region. Travelers can join in the revelry, immerse themselves in local traditions, and create lasting memories of vibrant summer nights.

- Exploring Coastal Gems and Island Escapes

Calabria's coastal towns and islands become the focal points of summer tourism. Tropea, known as the "Jewel of the

Tyrrhenian Coast," captures the hearts of visitors with its stunning cliffs, clear waters, and charming historic center. The Aeolian Islands, located off the northern coast of Calabria, beckon travelers with their volcanic landscapes and laid-back island atmosphere.

- Indulging in the Gastronomic Delights

Summer also offers a chance to indulge in the delectable flavors of Calabrian cuisine. Fresh seafood, sun-ripened fruits, and aromatic herbs take center stage in dishes that celebrate the region's bountiful harvest. From the famous spicy spread 'Nduja to refreshing gelato, the culinary offerings of Calabria delight the taste buds of travelers.

Autumn (September to November): Embracing Calabria's Tranquil Charm and Harvest Bounty

As summer gradually gives way to autumn, Calabria undergoes a graceful transformation, trading the summer fervor for a sense of tranquility and abundance. From September to November, the region experiences a more serene atmosphere as the temperatures become milder, making it an ideal time for exploring the cultural heritage, savoring the flavors of the land, and embracing the vibrant hues of the fall foliage.

- A Symphony of Colors in the Landscape

Autumn paints the landscape of Calabria with warm and earthy tones. The countryside is awash with shades of red, orange, and gold as the vineyards and orchards prepare for the harvest. The national parks, too, become a tapestry of colors as the forests of Sila and Aspromonte adopt an enchanting allure.

- Harvest Season and Gastronomic Delights

Autumn is a culinary delight in Calabria, as the region's fertile lands yield a bountiful harvest of fruits, vegetables, and olives. It is the time of the year to indulge in seasonal delicacies, such as figs, chestnuts, and the renowned red onions of Tropea. Local wineries celebrate the grape harvest with festive events, and visitors have the opportunity to taste exquisite wines made from traditional grape varieties.

- Cultural Explorations and Traditional Events

With the summer crowds waning, autumn offers a more intimate setting to explore the historical gems of Calabria. Wander through the cobblestone streets of medieval towns and immerse yourself in the region's rich cultural heritage. September marks the beginning of various religious festivals and traditional events, allowing visitors to witness the genuine expressions of faith and local customs.

Winter (December to February): Discovering Calabria's Winter Wonderland and Coastal Serenity

While winter might not be the conventional high season for tourism, Calabria takes on a different kind of charm during the colder months. From December to February, the region embraces its quieter side, inviting travelers to discover the serene beauty of its inland mountains and experience the coastal towns in their more tranquil state.

- Winter Wonders in the Inland Mountains

Inland Calabria transforms into a winter wonderland during the colder months. The mountains of Sila and Aspromonte are blanketed in snow, attracting winter sports enthusiasts to their slopes for skiing, snowboarding, and other winter activities. The idyllic mountain villages become picturesque retreats where visitors can cozy up by the fireplace and relish the peacefulness of the snowy landscapes.

- Coastal Towns in Tranquility

Along the coast, the beach towns embrace a slower pace, providing a genuine taste of local life. Winter is an excellent time for those seeking a more authentic experience, as the absence of large crowds allows for meaningful interactions with the warm-hearted locals. Stroll along the deserted beaches, savoring the fresh sea breeze and contemplating the beauty of the Mediterranean in its tranquil state.

- Festive Spirit and Holiday Celebrations

Calabria's festive spirit comes alive during the winter season, with towns and villages hosting Christmas markets, nativity scenes, and traditional holiday events. From December through January, the region celebrates various religious festivities and cultural traditions that create an atmosphere of warmth and togetherness.

Conclusion

Calabria's distinct seasons offer an array of experiences and delights for every traveler. Whether you choose to explore the blooming landscapes of spring, bask in the

Mediterranean sun of summer, embrace the autumn harvest, or discover the serene beauty of winter, Calabria's best-kept secret will undoubtedly leave a lasting impression on your heart and soul. Embrace the spirit of Calabria as you embark on an unforgettable journey through this enchanting region of Southern Italy.

9.2 Getting Around: Transportation in Calabria

Navigating Calabria is relatively straightforward, thanks to its well-developed transportation network. Here are the primary modes of transportation available in the region:

Trains: Exploring Calabria's Scenic Railways and Convenient Connectivity

One of the most convenient and picturesque ways to travel through Calabria is by train. Trenitalia, the national railway operator in Italy, operates the main train services that connect the major cities and towns in the region. Traveling by train allows you to enjoy the stunning landscapes of Calabria and experience the seamless connectivity between different regions.

Convenient Connectivity and City Hopping

Calabria's train network offers an efficient means of transportation between the region's urban centers and towns. The trains are well-maintained, comfortable, and provide a relaxing journey for passengers. Whether you are traveling from the bustling city of Reggio Calabria to the historic town of Cosenza or heading to the coastal gem of

Tropea, the train system ensures smooth and timely connectivity.

Scenic Journeys through Breathtaking Landscapes

The train rides in Calabria offer passengers breathtaking views of the region's diverse landscapes. As the train winds its way through valleys, crosses bridges, and skirts along the coastline, travelers are treated to vistas of lush mountains, vineyards, and the sparkling sea. The journey through Calabria's national parks, such as Sila and Aspromonte, is a particularly awe-inspiring experience, as the train meanders through forests and mountain passes.

Plan Ahead for Remote Areas

While the train network is well-developed in Calabria, some of the more remote areas might not have frequent train connections. Therefore, it is essential to plan ahead and check the train schedules to ensure you can reach your desired destinations. In certain cases, buses or other modes of transportation may be required for the last leg of the journey to explore hidden gems that lie off the beaten path.

Buses: Immerse Yourself in Local Culture and Scenic Routes

Local and regional buses complement the train network in Calabria, providing access to destinations that may not be easily reachable by train. Buses serve as a reliable mode of transportation, connecting urban centers, rural areas, and charming villages. Traveling by bus offers a unique opportunity to immerse yourself in the local culture, interact with locals, and witness the everyday life of Calabrians.

Convenient Intra-City Transportation

Within cities and towns, buses offer a convenient way to navigate through the bustling streets and vibrant neighborhoods. Whether you're exploring the historic centers of Catanzaro or taking in the seaside charm of Tropea, buses provide a cost-effective and efficient means of getting around.

Scenic Routes and Off-the-Beaten-Path Adventures

Buses in Calabria often take scenic routes that offer passengers breathtaking views of the surrounding landscapes. As you traverse through the hilly terrains and coastal cliffs, the journey becomes an adventure in itself. Many routes pass by picturesque vineyards, olive groves, and idyllic countryside, giving you a glimpse of the region's natural beauty.

Car Rentals: Embrace Flexibility and Discover Hidden Gems

For travelers seeking ultimate flexibility in exploring Calabria, renting a car is an excellent option. Rental agencies are readily available at airports, major cities, and tourist hubs, allowing visitors to embark on self-guided adventures to remote villages, lesser-known attractions, and the charming countryside.

Explore at Your Own Pace

Having a car allows you to set your own itinerary and explore the region at your preferred pace. You can take spontaneous detours to off-the-beaten-path destinations, discover hidden viewpoints, and stop at local eateries to savor traditional Calabrian delicacies.

Access Hidden Gems and Scenic Routes

Calabria is replete with hidden gems that may not be easily accessible by public transportation. With a rental car, you can venture into the heart of the national parks, discover secluded beaches, and reach historic landmarks tucked away in the countryside.

Scenic Coastal Drives and Panoramic Vistas

The coastal drives in Calabria are renowned for their scenic beauty and panoramic vistas. Driving along the coastline, you'll be treated to spectacular views of the turquoise waters, rocky cliffs, and charming seaside villages. The famous "Costa degli Dei" (Coast of the Gods) road between Tropea and Nicotera is a must-drive route that offers awe-inspiring views of the Tyrrhenian Sea.

Ferries: Expanding Your Journey to Island Escapes and Sicily

As Calabria is surrounded by the Ionian and Tyrrhenian Seas, ferries provide an enticing option for travelers to explore nearby islands and even reach Sicily. Ferry services offer a scenic and enjoyable way to expand your journey and experience the wonders of the surrounding seas.

Aeolian Islands: A Tropical Paradise

The Aeolian Islands, a volcanic archipelago off the northern coast of Calabria, are accessible by ferry and are a tropical paradise for nature lovers and adventurers. Each island has its unique charm, from the fiery Stromboli, known for its regular volcanic activity, to the tranquil Lipari, offering beautiful beaches and historic sites.

Sicily: A Fascinating Island Adventure

Calabria's proximity to Sicily makes it a convenient starting point for travelers wishing to explore the largest island in the Mediterranean. Ferries connect Calabria to various ports in Sicily, including Messina, Milazzo, and Palermo. From there, you can delve into Sicily's rich history, cultural heritage, and awe-inspiring landscapes, from the historic city of Taormina to the towering Mount Etna.

Conclusion

Transportation options in Calabria cater to every type of traveler, offering convenient connectivity, scenic journeys, and opportunities for exploration. Whether you prefer the convenience of trains, the immersion of buses, the flexibility of car rentals, or the expansion of ferry journeys, each mode of transportation provides a unique perspective of this captivating region in Southern Italy. Embrace the diverse modes of transportation available in Calabria as you embark on a journey of discovery, beauty, and cultural richness that the region has to offer.

9.3 Accommodation Options: Hotels, B&Bs, and More

Calabria offers a variety of accommodation options to suit different preferences and budgets. Whether you prefer luxury hotels, cozy B&Bs, or unique stays, you'll find something to match your needs:

Hotels: Luxurious Retreats and Charming Hideaways with Sea Views

Calabria welcomes travelers with a wide array of hotels that cater to different preferences and budgets. Whether you seek opulence and grandeur or a quaint and intimate setting, the region's hotels offer a delightful range of accommodations that enhance your overall experience of exploring Italy's best-kept secret.

Luxurious Resorts with Breathtaking Sea Views

For those seeking a luxurious and indulgent experience, Calabria's coastal areas boast a selection of high-end resorts that command breathtaking views of the azure sea. These luxurious retreats provide a harmonious blend of modern comforts and natural beauty, offering guests a chance to unwind and rejuvenate in a serene and exclusive environment.

Amenities for Ultimate Relaxation

Hotels in Calabria often feature an array of amenities, including inviting swimming pools, spa facilities, and wellness centers. After a day of exploration, guests can retreat to the comforts of their hotels to enjoy rejuvenating spa treatments, lounge by the poolside, or simply soak in the stunning vistas from the comfort of their rooms.

Charming Boutique Hotels in Historic Towns

In the heart of Calabria's historic towns and cities, charming boutique hotels offer a more intimate and immersive experience. These carefully curated accommodations often occupy historic buildings, reflecting the region's rich heritage and culture. Staying in a boutique hotel allows travelers to immerse themselves in the local ambiance and be within walking distance of iconic landmarks and cultural attractions.

Personalized Service and Local Hospitality

At Calabria's hotels, guests are greeted with warm Italian hospitality, ensuring that their stay is comfortable and memorable. The staff at these establishments take pride in delivering personalized service, attending to guests' needs with care and attention to detail, making the overall stay an unforgettable experience.

Bed and Breakfasts (B&Bs): A Cozy Home-Away-From-Home Experience

For travelers seeking a more intimate and personalized experience, bed and breakfasts (B&Bs) provide an enchanting stay in the heart of Calabria. Often family-run, B&Bs offer a warm and welcoming atmosphere, creating a sense of home away from home for their guests.

Welcoming Ambiance and Local Insights

The hosts of B&Bs are passionate about sharing their love for Calabria and its unique culture. They are excellent sources of local knowledge, providing insider tips on the best places to explore, dine, and experience the authentic essence of the region.

Urban Centers and Countryside Retreats

B&Bs can be found in both urban centers and idyllic countryside settings. In the historic towns, these accommodations may occupy charming old buildings, exuding a rustic charm that complements the surrounding architecture. In the tranquil countryside, B&Bs provide a serene retreat, offering guests an opportunity to reconnect with nature and escape the hustle and bustle of city life.

Delicious Homemade Breakfasts

One of the highlights of staying at a B&B is the delicious homemade breakfast served each morning. Guests are treated to a delightful spread of fresh local produce, traditional pastries, and aromatic coffee, setting the perfect tone for a day of exploration and discovery in Calabria.

Agriturismos: Embracing Rural Calabria and Authentic Culinary Experiences

For travelers seeking an immersive and authentic experience in rural Calabria, agriturismos offer a unique opportunity to connect with the region's agricultural traditions. These accommodations are typically located on working farms, allowing guests to experience firsthand the bounty of the land and indulge in authentic local cuisine.

The Beauty of Rural Living

Staying at an agriturismo allows travelers to experience the rustic beauty of Calabria's countryside. Surrounded by rolling hills, vineyards, and olive groves, guests are transported to a world of tranquility and natural splendor.

Authentic Culinary Experiences

The agriturismos take pride in serving guests farm-to-table meals, showcasing the region's freshest and finest ingredients. Guests can savor traditional Calabrian dishes, often prepared with recipes handed down through generations, and pair them with local wines produced on the farm.

Hands-On Farm Activities

At agriturismos, guests have the chance to participate in hands-on farm activities, such as harvesting fruits, tending to the animals, or learning traditional agricultural practices. These immersive experiences offer a deeper understanding of Calabria's rural lifestyle and the dedication of its farmers.

Holiday Rentals: A Home Away From Home

For travelers seeking an extended stay in Calabria or those traveling with a group, holiday rentals and vacation homes provide a home-away-from-home experience. These accommodations offer the comfort and privacy of a fully furnished house or apartment, making them ideal for families or groups of friends looking to share their travel experience.

Ample Space and Kitchen Facilities

Holiday rentals provide ample space, giving guests the freedom to relax and unwind in a private setting. Many rentals come equipped with kitchen facilities, allowing guests to prepare their own meals using fresh local ingredients from nearby markets.

Flexibility and Independence

Staying in a holiday rental offers travelers the flexibility to create their own schedule and explore Calabria at their leisure. Whether it's a lazy morning spent enjoying a leisurely breakfast or a late evening gathering on a private terrace, holiday rentals embrace a sense of freedom and independence.

Discovering Hidden Corners

Renting a vacation home often places travelers in residential neighborhoods, providing a unique opportunity to immerse themselves in local life and discover hidden corners of Calabria that may not be easily accessible to tourists.

Conclusion

Calabria's diverse range of accommodations caters to the varying preferences and desires of travelers, ensuring a memorable and comfortable stay in this captivating region of Southern Italy. Whether you choose to embrace the luxury of hotels, the charm of B&Bs, the authenticity of agriturismos, or the home-away-from-home experience of holiday rentals, each option enriches your journey through the enchanting landscapes and cultural treasures of Calabria. As you embark on your Calabria escapades, the region's accommodations become not merely places to rest, but integral parts of your experience, shaping cherished memories that will stay with you long after your departure.

Unique Stays: Calabria also offers unique and unconventional accommodations, such as castle stays, ancient farmhouses, and eco-lodges. These options provide a memorable and distinctive experience.

9.4 Basic Phrases and Vocabulary

As with any travel destination, knowing a few basic phrases and vocabulary in the local language can enhance your interactions with locals and show your appreciation for their culture. In Calabria, the majority of people speak Italian, but you'll also encounter the Calabrian dialect. Here are some essential phrases and words to get you started:

- Hello - Ciao / Salve
- Good morning - Buongiorno
- Good afternoon - Buon pomeriggio
- Good evening - Buonasera
- Goodbye - Arrivederci / Addio
- Thank you - Grazie
- Please - Per favore
- Yes - Sì
- No - No
- Excuse me / Sorry - Scusa / Mi scusi
- I don't understand - Non capisco
- How much is this? - Quanto costa?
- Where is...? - Dove si trova...?
- Bathroom - Bagno
- Help! - Aiuto!
- Water - Acqua
- Food - Cibo
- Restaurant - Ristorante / Trattoria

- Coffee - Caffè
- Wine - Vino
- Beer - Birra
- Breakfast - Colazione
- Lunch - Pranzo
- Dinner - Cena
- Delicious - Delizioso
- Cheers! - Salute!
- I love Calabria - Amo la Calabria
- Beautiful - Bellissimo / Bellissima
- Beach - Spiaggia
- Sea - Mare
- Mountain - Montagna
- Village - Villaggio / Paese
- City - Città
- Church - Chiesa
- Castle - Castello
- Historic center - Centro storico
- Market - Mercato
- Shopping - Shopping
- Excursion - Escursione
- Ticket - Biglietto
- Bus - Autobus
- Train - Treno
- Airport - Aeroporto
- Hotel - Hotel
- Bed and Breakfast - Bed and Breakfast (B&B)
- Agriturismo - Agriturismo (accommodation on a working farm)
- Beach resort - Resort sulla spiaggia

- Car rental - Noleggio auto
- Museum - Museo
- Park - Parco

Please note that the official language of Italy, including Calabria, is Italian. However, you may also encounter the Calabrian dialect, especially in more rural areas. These basic phrases and vocabulary will help you communicate effectively and show appreciation for the local culture during your travels in Calabria.

Remember, locals appreciate any effort you make to speak their language, even if it's just a few basic phrases. A warm smile and a friendly attitude will always go a long way in creating positive interactions during your Calabria escapades.

CONCLUSION

Embracing the Spirit of Calabria

Calabria, with its captivating landscapes and warm-hearted people, holds a unique spirit that weaves a spell of enchantment on all who have the privilege of visiting. In this chapter, we embark on a journey beyond the surface and dive into the very essence of Calabria, discovering the intangible qualities that make it so extraordinarily special. As you set foot on this ancient land, you'll immediately sense an irresistible pull towards its rich heritage, time-honored traditions, and the genuine warmth of its inhabitants. Prepare to be enthralled by the essence of Calabria and embrace a world where culture, history, and natural beauty converge to create an unforgettable experience.

The spirit of Calabria is deeply rooted in its ancient history and cultural legacy. Tracing its origins back to the days of Magna Graecia, this region was once a hub of Greek colonization, leaving behind a significant impact on its language, architecture, and customs. As we explore Calabria's historic sites and ruins, we begin to comprehend the profound connection it holds with the past. From the impressive archaeological sites of Locri and Scolacium to the majestic medieval castles dotting the landscape, the echoes of centuries past resonate throughout the region, beckoning travelers to immerse themselves in its storied past.

Beyond the tangible historical remnants, the heart of Calabria lies in the spirited nature of its people. Known for their warmth, hospitality, and strong sense of community, the Calabrians are eager to share their cherished traditions and authentic way of life with visitors. In Calabria, it is not just about seeing, but about participating and becoming part of the community. Whether it's joining in the lively celebrations of a local festival or savoring a traditional meal prepared with love and care, you'll quickly find yourself embraced as one of their own.

As you traverse the diverse landscapes of Calabria, you'll witness how the natural beauty further enhances its spirit. From the azure waters lapping against the sandy shores of the Ionian and Tyrrhenian coasts to the breathtaking vistas of the Sila and Aspromonte mountain ranges, Calabria's landscapes are both awe-inspiring and humbling. Nature lovers and adventure enthusiasts alike will find solace in the lush national parks, where dense forests, crystal-clear lakes, and charming villages await exploration.

The soul of Calabria also lives in its vibrant culture, which is celebrated through captivating music, dance, and art. Traditional folk music, often accompanied by the sounds of tambourines and bagpipes, fills the air during festivals and gatherings, inviting you to clap your hands and join the dance. The intricate handicrafts, like the delicate Pizzo lace and the vibrant ceramic pottery, showcase the artistic prowess of Calabria's skilled artisans, each piece a testament to the region's creativity and craftsmanship.

Furthermore, Calabria's culinary offerings are a true reflection of its soul. From the fiery 'Nduja, a spicy spreadable salami, to the hearty Cuzzupa, a traditional Easter bread, each dish tells a story of regional flavors and ancient traditions passed down through generations. Savoring these authentic delicacies is a celebration of

Calabria's culinary heritage and an opportunity to connect with the essence of its people.

In the welcoming atmosphere of Calabria, you'll find a sense of belonging that transcends borders and cultures. It's a place where strangers become friends, and where time seems to slow down, allowing you to savor every moment. The spirit of Calabria beckons you to immerse yourself fully, to listen to the tales whispered by ancient ruins, to dance with joy in the midst of colorful festivals, and to bask in the warmth of its people's smiles.

As you embrace the spirit of Calabria, its enchantment will weave itself into the very fabric of your being. You'll leave with a heart full of cherished memories and a soul forever touched by the magic of this hidden gem in Southern Italy. Open your heart to the wonders that Calabria offers, and you'll find a piece of yourself forever entwined with its spirit, beckoning you to return time and time again.

Responsible Travel: Supporting Local Communities

As responsible travelers, we hold a profound responsibility to understand and acknowledge the impact our journeys can have on the places we visit. In this section, we focus on the paramount importance of sustainable tourism in the enchanting region of Calabria. Beyond merely admiring its beauty, we delve into the intricate relationship between tourism and the well-being of local communities and the environment.

Tourism, when approached responsibly, has the potential to bring numerous benefits to the people of Calabria. It can stimulate economic growth, provide employment opportunities, and foster cultural exchange. However, we also shed light on the potential negative consequences of uncontrolled tourism, such as overdevelopment, environmental degradation, and cultural commodification. By understanding both sides of the coin, we aim to foster a sense of mindfulness among travelers, encouraging them to be proactive agents of positive change.

Throughout the pages of this chapter, we highlight the commendable efforts made by various organizations and individuals dedicated to preserving Calabria's rich cultural heritage and safeguarding its precious natural resources. From local community initiatives to government-backed projects, these conservation endeavors serve as beacons of hope, ensuring that future generations can continue to experience Calabria's authenticity and magnificence.

One of the essential aspects of sustainable tourism is recognizing and respecting the traditional practices and customs of the local communities. We encourage travelers to engage with the residents, listen to their stories, and partake in their festivities with genuine appreciation and respect. By doing so, you not only gain a deeper understanding of the region's heritage but also contribute to the preservation of its cultural identity.

The protection of Calabria's pristine environment is of paramount importance. In this section, we also delve into the significance of eco-friendly practices during your travels. From minimizing waste and conserving water to supporting businesses that prioritize sustainable practices, there are numerous ways you can reduce your environmental impact and become an advocate for a cleaner, greener Calabria.

Supporting the local economy is another integral aspect of responsible tourism. We encourage travelers to patronize locally-owned businesses, artisans, and restaurants that showcase the region's authentic flavors and crafts. By choosing to buy locally-made souvenirs and products, you contribute directly to the livelihoods of the people who call Calabria home.

As you journey through the pages of this section, you'll discover a multitude of ways you can actively contribute to the well-being of Calabria and leave a positive footprint during your travels. Whether it's participating in volunteer programs, beach clean-ups, or supporting cultural preservation projects, each action, no matter how small, can make a meaningful difference.

In the end, embracing sustainable tourism in Calabria is not just about being mindful during your visit; it's about forging a connection with the land and its people, becoming a conscious ambassador for positive change. By adopting a responsible mindset, you ensure that the allure of Calabria remains intact for generations to come, leaving a lasting legacy of love and respect for this hidden gem of Southern Italy.

Let this section serve as an empowering guide for responsible travel, inspiring you to explore Calabria with a sense of purpose, leaving behind more than just footprints in the sand. Together, we can preserve the essence of Calabria's spirit and contribute to the preservation of its timeless beauty and cultural heritage for the world to cherish.

Saying Goodbye: Fond Farewells to Calabria

As the final chapter of our journey through Calabria unfolds, we find ourselves grappling with the bittersweet reality that all adventures must eventually come to an end. However, the memories we've created and the experiences that have imprinted on our hearts will forever remain with us, treasured like precious gems in the treasure trove of our minds.

Throughout this travel guide, we've embarked on a captivating exploration of Calabria's landscapes, culture, and people. We've witnessed the sun rise over the stunning coastal horizons, traversed ancient cobblestone streets, and indulged in the tantalizing flavors of Calabrian cuisine. Yet, it is the meaningful connections forged with the locals and the land that have made this journey truly extraordinary.

In this final chapter, we invite you to join us in reflecting on the heartwarming stories of fellow travelers who have encountered the true essence of Calabria. Tales of chance encounters with friendly locals who shared heartfelt conversations over cups of rich espresso or impromptu dances during village festivals. These stories epitomize the magic of travel, where strangers become friends, and the world becomes a tapestry of shared experiences.

Leaving Calabria physically is undoubtedly a moment tinged with nostalgia and a touch of melancholy. Yet, as we bid farewell to this enchanting land, we come to realize that the spirit of Calabria will forever remain intertwined with our own. The memories of sun-kissed days spent on the shores of its turquoise waters and evenings filled with laughter in bustling piazzas will continue to bring warmth to our souls, no matter where our future journeys may lead.

As we depart, we offer you a handful of tips on how to carry a piece of Calabria home with you. Souvenirs may serve as tangible reminders of your adventure, whether it be a locally crafted pottery piece or a traditional piece of Calabrian jewelry. These items hold not only the beauty of the region but also the stories of the artisans who lovingly created them.

The flavors of Calabria can also journey home with you through cherished recipes you've sampled during your stay. Perhaps you've delighted in the exquisite simplicity of a freshly-made pasta dish or experienced the fiery zing of 'Nduja that awakened your taste buds. Bringing these culinary delights into your own kitchen allows you to recreate the magic of Calabria and share it with loved ones.

Yet, beyond tangible keepsakes, the most significant mementos of Calabria reside in your heart and memory. The laughter shared with newfound friends, the awe of beholding a breathtaking sunset over the horizon, and the moments of peace found in the heart of nature all become cherished memories to hold close.

As we say farewell to Calabria, we do not part forever but rather bid it "arrivederci" - until we meet again. For, in the grand tapestry of our lives, this journey is but a thread, and the spirit of Calabria will always remain woven into the fabric of our beings. As you continue on your life's path, carry the lessons, the beauty, and the joy of Calabria with you, and may it inspire you to embark on many more adventures, each one imbued with the same wonder and reverence for the world around us. Safe travels, and until we reunite once more on the road less traveled.

Printed in Great Britain
by Amazon

42429195R00106